Preaching Unashamed

Preaching Unashamed

By

JOSEPH R. SIZOO

ABINGDON-COKESBURY PRESS

NEW YORK • NASHVILLE

PREACHING UNASHAMED

SET UP, PRINTED, AND BOUND BY THE
PARTHENON PRESS, AT NASHVILLE,
TENNESSEE, UNITED STATES OF AMERICA

Preface

IT IS A SINGULAR HONOR TO HAVE A PLACE IN THE LECTURES under the Jarrell Foundation at Emory University, and for that honor I would like to record my sincere gratitude. It is also a great privilege to have one's name linked to that gallant company of prophets who in the past have given so much dignity and meaning to this foundation, who have lifted the horizons of all who preach and brought a fresh urgency to the gospel we preach.

As one who has a part in this foundation I should like to give thanks to the memory of the one in whose name this lectureship is established. If in some way this book makes the task of the Christian ministry more joyful and compelling, you also will do well to give thanks to the one in whose name the foundation is established, who "endured, as seeing him who is invisible," and for whom "Nearer, My God, to Thee" is no longer a hymn of hope, but an eternal experience. I pause to salute his spirit.

JOSEPH R. SIZOO

Contents

I. WE ARE AMBASSADORS 9

II. THE SIGNS OF THE TIMES 30

III. THESE THINGS HAVE BEEN WRITTEN . . . 47

IV. RECONCILING THE WORLD UNTO HIMSELF 66

V. THE LOST SENSE OF WONDER 86

VI. THE PROTESTANT WITNESS 95

VII. WORDS ARE NOT ENOUGH 108

VIII. THE FELLOWSHIP OF THE CROSS 118

I. We Are Ambassadors

THE HISTORY OF THE CHRISTIAN CHURCH BEGAN THAT DAY when a handful of men stood up preaching. It was at Pentecost. In the upper room of a widow's home in Jerusalem, with the unction of the Holy Ghost upon them, the apostles stood up to bear witness to a new experience in faith. They gave a new emphasis and new interpretation to the Scriptures. With souls aglow and with the fires of faith burning in their hearts, they preached the light of the glory of God in the face of Jesus Christ. It was by expository preaching that the Christian Church was born.

From that upper room they went out into a world which hated them and a generation which hooted them, preaching the unsearchable riches of God's love. It seemed a fantastic mission and a forlorn hope. They had no publicity agent to advertise them and no political leaders to intercede for them. They were socially ostracized, politically disfranchised, ecclesiastically scorned, economically impoverished. The venom of religious bigotries, the casualness of political charlatans, the cruelty of social ostracism were their day-by-day experience. To hear them speak you would think they slept on beds of rose petals, when, as a matter of fact, they sang their hymns and bore their testimony in the sewers and catacombs of Rome. They endured, as seeing him who is invisible. Yet within three centuries they carried their gospel a thousand miles north and south, fifteen hundred miles east and west. Within three centuries one of their number became emperor. They carried the gates of an empire from their hinges, and the Christian faith became the established religion of the time. They bore the testimony of a good conscience and conquered in the fight. They stood before the world unashamed and unafraid. Their robes were made white in the blood of the Lamb.

In a letter of Jerome written in A.D. 403 there is this illuminating paragraph:

> Even in Rome itself paganism is left in solitude. The Egyptian Serapis has become a Christian. The Huns have learned the Psalter. The chilly Cynthians are warmed by the faith. Every pagan temple in Rome is covered with cobwebs. They who once were the gods of the nation remain under their leaking, lonely roofs with horned owls and other birds of the night.

Nothing in all history can match the miraculous growth and the amazing expansion of the fellowship of Jesus.

So the early centuries passed and there came the dark ages. The Visigoths under Alaric followed by the Huns under Attila swept across the Danube and turned civilization upside down and inside out. They reached the very gates of Rome. It seemed as if that world had come to an end. But Ulfilas crossed the Danube, entered the land of the Slav and preached. Vladimir, a Russian prince, was converted, and the cross of Christ was set up in the land of the Slav. Boniface tramped into the woods of the northern

10

countries of Europe preaching the good news of the Son of God, and established the Christian faith among the Teutonic peoples. Augustine crossed the English Channel, tramped the fields of Kent County to Canterbury, and in Britain was established the Christian Church. Through the evangel of the preacher the Church has expanded.

As the Church grew in power, it was threatened by its own success. Power is a dangerous thing to handle, even in religion. Power has often been the undoing of religious institutions. As the Church compromised in order to win, there crept in pagan customs, heartless ceremonials, and carnal practices which choked the life out of the Church. It was losing its soul. In that hour there arose a retired merchant, Peter Waldo by name, who cried out against the evils. Wycliffe lifted his voice against heartless formalities and John Huss was burned for preaching the visitations of divine judgment. So faded these morning stars one after another for seven generations. The voice of protest was silenced; the flames of a new faith were extinguished for two hundred years.

Then one night a German university student gave a party to a group of students and professors. At the end of a festive evening he announced, "Tonight you see me, tomorrow you will see me no more." And Martin Luther left his comfortable setting, fought for his soul, and after endless penance and mortification and a pilgrimage to Rome, nailed his ninety-five theses on the eve of All Saint's Day to the doors of his parish church and walked into the world to preach anew, "The just shall live by faith." By the

11

preaching of the Word was the Reformation born. These forebears of ours preferred to worship God on the bleak hillsides with souls aglow rather than bow before golden altars in a worship without soul. So from Isaiah to Washington Gladden, from Francis to Kagawa, from Paul and Chrysostom through Luther, Calvin, and Wesley to Phillips Brooks, by the preaching of God-filled men has the Church of Christ advanced and the Kingdom marched on to its predestined triumph.

It is a singular and significant fact that all the revivals of religion have come to pass through preaching. The resurgence of faith is indissolubly linked to this vibrant and vital witness. When Isaiah stood up to preach, a whole new concept of holiness was born in the earth. When Jeremiah walked out of the fields of Anathoth to prophesy, a new morality came to a whole nation. When Amos left his plow in the furrows of Tekoa to preach, there emerged a new social justice. When Augustine proclaimed the Holy City, there came with it the dawn of a new conscience. When Francis went up and down the village streets preaching, there came a new compassion for the poor and underprivileged. Through the preaching of Luther there blossomed in the earth a spiritual emancipation. The preaching of Calvin brought into being the birth of modern democracy. Through the preaching of John Wesley there was ushered in the age of the common man. A new day always dawns for the world when from among the faithful remnant there come those whose feet have been "shod with the preparation of the gospel," whose words and lives bear witness to the truth that is in Jesus Christ. We shall never recover our interest in preaching until we find again its importance in history.

All that is coming back. This is the age of preaching. The sermon is coming back into its own. For many years the common and current notion has prevailed that the minister was a sort of glorified promoter; a clever public-relations man; if possible, an able athlete; always a glad-hander and a professional joiner; of course, a leader of all kinds of clubs, crusades, and causes; a scintillating after-dinner speaker, not too saintly, and always terribly popular. But the Church suddenly awakened to find that something had gone out of that minister which it gave him no time to keep. Their lamps often went out. That day is now past, if it ever should have come. We have struck bottom on all that. People are coming to church, if they come at all, to hear the voice of a prophet, to look into the face of a man who has been alone with God, to hear someone who has meditated in the night watches with the Almighty, who can point them once again to the keeper of the lights and the Saviour of their souls. When John Chrysostom, perhaps the greatest preacher in the Christian Church, was banished from his beloved city of Constantinople by godless leaders who had been stunned by his sharp rebuke, the people said, "Better that Constantinople cease to be than that John Chrysostom should cease preaching." Something of that is coming back in our time.

When preaching is vital and vibrant, it becomes a living witness and something always comes of it. It is not simply an appeal to the aesthetic tastes of an age, to its intellectual

13

acumen, nor to its imagination and memory, but to its conscience and to its will. It is truth lit up by the fire of the soul. One of the distinguished Presbyterian divines of the last generation was Mark Matthews, more familiarly known as the "tall pine of the Sierras." A lawyer in Seattle who attended his church saw one morning, sitting near him, a charwoman who scrubbed the floors in his office. Somewhat surprised, he asked her the next day if she had been at the service. When she assured him that she had been there, the lawyer replied, "But Matthews is a very scholarly person; could you understand what he said?" To this she replied, "Oh no, I could not understand him, but he always washes clean the gutters of my life." That is the business of preaching.

Jonathan Edwards was very nearsighted. As he stood up to preach, he held a candle in his left hand and his manuscript close to his eyes in the right hand, yet he shook New England. Thomas Chalmers read his sermons word for word. They were rarely less than two hours in length, and he read them poorly. Yet people walked out of his church with lives made radiant and transformed, for it seemed to them as if they walked with God. That is the romance of preaching.

William Temple, the late archbishop of Canterbury, whose untimely death left such a hole in the sky, concludes his book *Christianity and Social Order* with this sentence: "I should give a false impression of my own convictions if I did not here add that there is no hope of establishing a more Christian social order except through the labour and

sacrifice of those in whom the Spirit of Christ is active."
That has been the proud role of the preacher in history.

But while there is coming into being a new attitude to
the importance and place of preaching, it must also be said
that there is much criticism of it today. Many people are
disappointed with present-day preachers. For one reason
or another our age is becoming quite critical of the preacher.
George Bernard Shaw is reported to have made the following observation about preaching: "Some preaching is like
wine: it has color and sparkle, but does no permanent
good; some is like drinking coffee: it stimulates, but does
not nourish; some is like carbonated water: a fuss over
nothing; some is like spring water: good, but hard to get."

For some years I have been a member of a small com-
mittee which reviews and selects the so-called best sermons
of the year. About four thousand of these sermons are sent
in. After going over these sermons, one cannot refrain
from saying there is too much shoddy preaching today.
Whatever may be the reasons, however deserving or unworthy may be the criticism toward modern preaching, of
one thing we may be sure: We must make ourselves much
more effective if we are to win the confidence of our day.
We must take ourselves in hand and, after careful self-
analysis, inquire how we may increase our effectiveness
that in the end we may become good ministers of Jesus
Christ.

It is quite true, of course, that preaching can never be
standardized. No person can lay down laws which if
meticulously observed will make great sermons or good

preaching. In the last analysis preaching is the attempt to state a religious experience and to make it so compelling that you will win people to it. Of necessity, therefore, it cannot be standardized.

Ministers are not made; they are born. Since becoming identified with a theological seminary, I have given much thought and time to finding students for the ministry. One of the perils of the Church is that it has not given sufficient care or concern to finding ministers, let alone training them. There was a time when the average boy from the Christian home of means went to the average college to become either a doctor, a lawyer, or a minister. Now and again some would tumble over into some other profession, but as a rule they did not. On that basis the Church could always count on its quota of ministers. All that has changed. This is a scientific age. Modern industry has gone into the colleges and universities to secure the most outstanding students. Indeed big business is going into secondary schools and offering scholarships to the most likely students, paying for their education in some technical school, and so training them for business. I do not blame the world of industry for this procedure, but the result of all this is that the Church often gets what is left. We need desperately a strategy to challenge these men.

Someone asked me some time ago how I happened to become a minister. If someone had told me when I went off to college that one day I would be a minister, I would have said the man should be psychoanalyzed. I went to college to prepare for medicine and had already enrolled my name in a well-known medical school. All my college work, therefore, was in that direction. But as time went on, for some reason I became exceedingly restless. Finally, at the end of my junior year, I remember well sitting alone with my mother late one warm June night on the veranda of our humble home in a midwestern city. I told her that I was not going to be a doctor, and she wanted to know what I was going to be. I told her I had decided to become a minister. She said nothing for some time. Then I broke the silence with a question, "Are you not glad?" To which she replied, "Of course I am." Then I asked her if she was surprised. She put her arm around my shoulders and said: "Listen Joe, long before you came, while I was carrying you, I went to my knees one night and prayed, 'God, if it is to be a boy, make him a minister.' I have never ceased to pray that prayer, and I have never doubted that it would end this way." You see, ministers are not made; they are born. It is an affair of an individual with his God.

Have you ever thought that to whatever God has given life, to that he has given individuality? A thousand leaves hang on the trees in oak forests, but every leaf differs from every other leaf in texture and design. A million stars will shine out of the night sky, but every star differs from every other star in glory. So it is with preaching. It is an affair of the individual. God makes every minister after a different mold, and when he has made the minister, he breaks the mold. All we can do is to share with one another our common experiences. That is what I propose to do. I will tell you frankly and simply what methods and procedures in preaching fit into my life. While they are valid for me, they may not be valid for you. Perhaps they will not even work in your life. But they work in mine, and I want to share with you the convictions which have been born of these experiences.

Let me, therefore, at the very outset place before you my credentials. To begin with I am an immigrant. I was something over six years of age when my father brought all of us to this country out of the Old World. I know something of the dilemmas and the psychological problems which work so deeply and fiercely among immigrant families. I know what it is to be forced to live in a foreign neighborhood with a feeling that you are not wanted. I know what it is to belong to a group in whom politicians are interested only in so far as they can exploit them. I know what it is to be compelled to live in areas where improvements are always last to come, where the schools are always poorest, and where the demagogue is always working overtime. I know something of the emotional tensions and maladjustments which follow in the wake of an immigrant family. You will find the problem of the immigrant coming to a focus in the great industrial centers of our country. The problem is far from solution. Regrettably, the Protestant Church has given it little concern. I know something, too, of the spiritual contributions immigrants have made to the molding of our American life.

My first parish was a small industrial community of about thirty-five hundred people. There I came to know intimately the economic, social, political, and religious problems and tensions which are much the same in every community. I came to understand the human element in the administration of the government, school, business, and the church. I saw at close range the day-by-day problems that arise in community life. This has stood me in good stead, for any great city is just an overgrown town. I have always thought that any young minister is fortunate who can begin his ministry in such a setting.

My second parish was a suburban community, the sort of a place where one comes to sleep at night and wash down a bit of toast with hot coffee as he runs for the 8:15. The commuter thinks in terms of the city where he works. He is apt to have little concern for the community of which he is a part save only to see to it that the taxes are kept down. In these suburban areas people are neither fish nor fowl. One often finds in such settings a strange kind of smugness and self-sufficiency which makes the work of a true minister difficult.

From there I went to Washington, the political capital of the world. I came to rub elbows with men who do the behind-the-scenes work in the life of our nation. I came to know something of diplomatic double talk, political chicanery, and international tight-rope walking. I saw men who did it all the time. I soon learned that politicians are quick to grant favors but slow to make amends. And I also met there other men who with vision and courage had dedicated themselves in great selflessness to the bringing in of a braver and better tomorrow. You will find more unselfishness and Christian integrity among our political leaders in a city like that than the rest of the country dreams of. I came to know something of the sensitiveness of this group to public opinion. I learned also the supreme lesson: the

19

power of the people in shaping the events of their own future.

Something over eleven years ago I turned my back upon those unforgettable years to come to New York. I did not want to leave, but I felt then, and still feel, that God led me there. Why, I do not know; but it is our business when he calls, to obey. It is hard to keep one's perspective in these seething centers where people are crowded together and live on top of one another. As Washington is the political capital, so New York is the financial center of the country, and perhaps the world. I came to know something of the power of money. When you stand up against ecclesiastical vested interests, you must be prepared to pay the price, for it leaves scars that never heal. It is in these cities that one comes to grip with life and that the battle for faith and freedom will have to be fought and won. Whether the Christian Church rises or falls will largely depend upon how it comes through the fires of these seething, relentless, and impersonal, industrial centers. Life, in these cities, is grim and ungloved, but it has at least the supreme virtue of being realistic.

Now I have come to the presidency of a historic theological seminary, having a share in finding and training men for the Christian Church. I am deeply convinced that this is the first and supreme test of the Church. Unless the forces of religion are led by men who know where and what the goal posts are; unless there come into the leadership of our time men who are God-conscious and Christ-filled, men with imagination and courage, willing to blaze new trails and take the blows, I see little hope for organized religion.

Out of all these experiences and settings there have come certain convictions which I want to share with you.

Let me begin by making, ever so briefly, this first observation. There is no substitute for preaching. We are to bear witness. There is in the Church a place for ceremony, pageantry, and ritual. One should not fear them where they can contribute to worship and the cultivation of reverence. There is room too for administration, technique, and organization. But in too many churches too much time is devoted just to keeping the wheels turning. Indeed, there are churches where one hears little beyond the rattling of ecclesiastical machinery. Now pageantry and organization and ritual have their place and may be helpful in bringing people face to face with God, but what this blundering world is seeking so desperately today is to look into the face of the man of God who has climbed the storm-swathed sides of Sinai saying, "Thus saith the Lord."

There is another deep conviction which has come to me through the years. There are certain things which a preacher must know. He must know his age—the times in which he lives, the world of which he is part, and the community in which his life is set. He must see and feel the tragedy and tears, the hopes and dreams, the dilemmas and disillusionments, the faith and the frustration of people. Again, the preacher must know his Book—the source of his power and inspiration, the Book through which man speaks to God

21

and God speaks to man. Then, too, the preacher must know his gospel. He is called to be an ambassador and deliver from the King of kings a message to the people of earth. He did not make that message, neither can he change it, neither can he disregard it. He must be able to give an account of the faith that is in him, and heed again the last message of Peter, "Be ready always to give to every man that asketh you a reason of the hope that is in you."

But most of all the preacher must know himself. Words do not mean very much these days. If words could change mankind, this world would be paradise. But words that are divorced from example and life fall upon dead ears. It is the man in whom words are incarnated who has a message for our time. The way he speaks about religion must conform to the way he lives with religion. If there is no relation between what he says and what he is, a cynical world will only walk away with increasing cynicism.

Let me make a third observation. Indeed, it is the underlying cause of the influence of the preacher. If we are to recover the importance of preaching and be worthy of those who have brought the Christian faith into being, there is one word which must come back into the preacher's day-by-day thinking. It is the word "compassion." We shall have little to say to the dilemmas and disillusionments of our age unless we approach them with a sense of divine concern. Among the Omaha Indians during the frontier times there was a strange custom. If an Indian left the bounds of the tribe and traveled for a little while within the areas of other tribes, on the night before he left home he would be compelled to sit with the chiefs of the tribe around the campfire. Just before the fire fell back into gray ash, he would be asked to stand, and there silhouetted against a dying flame, would be compelled to lift this prayer: "Great Spirit, help me never to judge another until I have walked two weeks in his moccasins." The true minister of Christ must learn to walk in other people's shoes. One of the ancient prophets wrote, "I sat where they sat." Of Moses it was recorded, "He went out unto his brethren, and looked on their burdens." We shall never recover the romance of preaching until there comes back this compassion.

That was the glory of the preaching ministry of Jesus. The most striking characteristic of his life was his approachableness. He identified himself with people. He shared with them their common lot. He became part of the life of his generation. He seemed to belong to them. Nothing that happened to people was foreign to him. He dragged the sorrows of his generation across his soul. He could not keep himself out of the welter and misery of men. Their problems were his problems, their dilemmas were his dilemmas, their pain was his anguish, their disappointments were his sorrow. At midnight it was a Hebrew scholar; at daybreak it was a foundering ship; at noonday it was a fallen girl at the well; in the afternoon it was a company of hungry unemployed. Across the threshold of his home in Capernaum there fell the shadows of the limping and the lame, the halt and the blind. And he healed them all. He identified himself with the paralytic who had just enough feeling to know pain. He became one with the lepers whose bodies writhed in anguish. He seemed to belong to the blind who stumbled

23

through the streets of eternal darkness. He cared what happened to the lily that had faded, the reed that was bent, the coin that was lost, the prodigal who had stepped across the threshold of indiscretion. He was the most compassionate man who ever lived.

There were two things Jesus did not know how to do. He did not know how to doubt, and he did not know how to hate. To the end of the end he lived with a love that would not let man go and with a faith that would not let God go. He was touched by the feelings of man's infirmity. He was always taking a towel and girding himself.

There can never be great preaching without great compassion. It is so easy to live comfortable lives, wrap ourselves up in the dry ice of calloused unconcern. We are prone to climb into ivory towers, look at the heartache of the world, say, "What a mess," and pull down the curtain upon it all. One day Dostoyevski wrote, "The only contribution which civilization has made is to increase man's capacity for pain." Unless we feel that pain and walk in that darkness with men, we can never hope to be worthy of the gospel we preach. Believe me, this blundering world is waiting for the sunrise of those men of God who see the sordid shambles, the pitiful disillusionments, the devastating injustices, and the dreadful cynicisms of the hour, not with callousness but with compassion; not with indifference but with interest.

I suppose the best known and most loved war correspondent of the last war was one familiarly known as Ernie Pyle. There is one sentence in the last dispatch which he sent before he left the European battle front. It is this:

"The hurt has finally become too great. Hating this business as much as I do, one becomes part of it. You leave something of yourself when you leave it." He spoke to the heart of a nation about the war because he had a great heart. That is needed in preaching.

Do you know Emile Cammaerts, who wrote a little book entitled *Upon This Rock*? He was poet laureate of Belgium. During the war, news came one day that his son, who was a flyer in the R.A.F., had been killed. In that hour of sorrow he sat down with himself and tried to think through a philosophy that would sustain him. He wrote his conclusions in this little book, a prose poem. He discovered that his eldest daughter, the strongest and finest Christian in the family, was becoming very weak. He spoke to her about it and asked why it was that she who was the strongest in the faith should seem so desolate. She replied, "It is not a question of strength, it is a question of realization. I never realized before what the Cross meant—we are sharing the responsibility for that suffering now, and the crucifixion goes on." There you have the secret of all great preaching and the one element which is fundamental to the witness the preacher bears.

It is not easy to keep your compassion in a world such as this. You always have to fight for it. When I went to New York eleven years ago, I determined that whatever I would do or not do I would try to keep my compassion. It is hard to keep it in certain settings, but I hope I have not lost it. You never solve problems by calling people names. There is enough fault finding in the everyday life without the minister of religion joining the anvil chorus on Sunday.

A few years ago I became greatly concerned about the increase of crime in New York, and I determined to find out why all this came to pass. There are about one and one-quarter million people each year in that city who are called to the courts for some offense. The average case load of the average judge in courts such as these in our country is about twenty-five hundred per year. The average case load of similar judges in that city is about thirty thousand.

I recall one day sitting with a judge on the bench when one of these unfortunates who had gone astray was in the witness chair. The man saw me sitting there, and he became very uneasy. I seemed to be his guilty conscience. When he left the witness chair and the court adjourned, I walked up to him and said, "Neighbor, why did you do this thing, anyway, and why don't you come through clean?" He turned to me and said, "I had come to believe that nobody cared any more." That is a dreadful judgment. Woe be to the minister who loses his compassion for blundering people.

One hears a great deal about being our brother's keeper. It is a commonplace slogan. And yet, I confess that sometimes it frightens me. What incalculable wrongs have been done, what autocracy has been established because a few men thought themselves or appointed themselves keepers of others! In the Christian philosophy we are not to be our brother's keeper, but our brother's brother; and that is different.

There is a vast difference between being a leader and a crusader. It is easy to be a crusader today; it is equally difficult to be a leader. A crusader is one who marches far in advance of people and is apt to lose touch with them. Indeed, he is so far in advance of people that he loses touch with them, and they lose touch with him. But a leader is one who walks in advance of his people but stays near enough to them so that he never loses sight of them, and they never lose sight of him. You may recall a Toonerville Trolley cartoon in which a citizen with his proverbial umbrella became angry with the motorman because the trolley didn't seem to progress very rapidly. So he walked up to the motorman and said, "Say, mister, can't you go any faster?" The motorman in shirt sleeves, with a gray beard, and proverbial corn-cob pipe, replied, "Oh yes, I can go faster, but I want to stay with the car." This, too, is part of the compassion of all great preaching. Dr. Santayana, the distinguished New England savant, was lecturing one day before a group of students at Harvard University. At the end of his lecture he said, "If it were given to me to look into the heart of a man, and I found there no good will I would say, 'You are not an American.'" Whether or no that is true, I have no desire to debate, but I do know it must be true of the minister.

At the turning of the nineteenth century there lived one of the great apostles of Christendom. His friends and his father called him mad. He was a very ordinary village preacher without much formal education. His health was such that doctors despaired of him. He was so poor that he lacked the necessities of life. He had to eke out his pitiful existence by mending shoes. But he had one consuming desire. It was to preach the story of God's love to the benighted people of India. He achieved his goal. For forty years he worked there without furlough. He opened the first church school in India, founded the first European-managed school, founded Serampore College. But most of all he preached the love of God. When Alexander Duff went to visit him, he begged him to say nothing about him, but much about his Saviour. When he died, they laid him in a grave at Serampore, over which there is a stone upon which he authorized these words to be placed:

William Carey, Born August 17, 1761, Died June 9, 1834
A wretched, poor and helpless worm
On Thy kind arms I fall

Let me quote from the principles which he laid down for himself and his brotherhood in a simple document entitled, "An enquiry—to use for the conversion of the Heathens." He ordered it to be read three times a year by each missionary in each station in their charge. I quote from it:

1. To set an infinite value on men's souls.
2. To abstain from whatever deepens India's prejudices.
3. To esteem and treat Indians always as equals.
4. To cultivate the spiritual gifts of the Indian brethren.
5. Let us bear hardness as soldiers of Jesus Christ.

This is the road and this is the direction the minister of Christ must travel if he is to be worthy of the inheritance into which he has entered, preaching the evangel, burning like a flame, shining like a torch, from hearts that are consumed with compassion.

Do you know Matthew Arnold's sonnet?

'Twas August, and the fierce sun overhead
Smote on the squalid squares of Bethnal Green,
And the pale weaver, through his window seen
In Spitalfields, looked thrice dispirited;

I met a preacher there I knew, and said:
"Ill and o'erworked, how fare you in this scene?"
"Bravely!" said he; "for I of late have been
Much cheer'd with thoughts of Christ, *the living bread.*"

O human soul! so long as thou canst so
Set up a mark of everlasting light,
Above the howling senses' ebb and flow,

To cheer thee, and to right thee if thou roam,
Not with lost toil thou labourest through the night!
Thou mak'st the heaven thou hop'st indeed thy home.

II. The Signs of the Times

I HAVE JUST FINISHED SAYING THAT THOSE WHO HAVE accomplished most for the kingdom of God have lived with a deep compassion. Indeed, the Christian ministry is the comradeship of the compassionate. Because I have certain political, economic, and social convictions is no reason why other people should hold these same political, economic, and social convictions. I may be right; they may be right. If I am right, I am duty-bound to convert them, but I have no right to slander them or shoot them. Without compassion we shall never stand before God and man unashamed.

But it must be an intelligent concern. There can be no great preaching without knowing the age to which you preach. All the great prophets of the past from Moses and Amos, through Paul to Wesley and Gladden understood their world, and because of that understanding of their world, they had a message for it. A physician cannot minister to a patient unless he knows the ailment. It is because we do not understand the trends and tensions of today that so much of preaching misses fire. It has no bearing upon life. It is as useless as to administer epecac for glaucoma or to apply splints to a man suffering from heartburn. If we are to have something to say to our age, we must first know it. Now it is possible to understand the age, at least in part. Modern methods of communication and transportation have so shrunk the surface of the earth that you can hold it in your hands and put your fingers all around it. What, then, are some of the characteristics of the age of which we must be aware if we are to preach unashamed and unafraid?

You do not have to keep your ear close to the ground very long or travel far or read much to discover that it is marked by moral instability. We have motion but not direction. Indeed, we are living in an age which is taking a moral tailspin. During the war the military often dropped paratroopers behind the enemy lines to destroy their communications. They soon discovered that the most effective method was to drop these men at intersections and change the road signs. As the enemy retreated, he often traveled in the wrong direction and ran into a cul-de-sac. He simply did not know where he was going. That is one of the obvious characteristics of today.

Integrity is almost a forgotten word. One does not hear it very often. Well-meaning but misguided people live with a pleasing illusion; and because the illusion is so pleasing, it is all the more deadly and fatal. It is this: that the enthusiasm for unselfishness generated by the war will be permanent. Many people have made themselves believe that the social restraint and self-disipline which the war engendered will continue in the post-war world. That is a dreadful illusion. There is no warrant for that conclusion in history. The Civil War, in the North, was followed by

31

a period of unbelievable political corruption, which struck an all-time low in the Tweed Ring of New York. The Napoleonic era was followed by an age of untutored nationalism and the cultivation of class-consciousness which persists and plagues us to this day. The First World War was followed by an era of so-called freedom. The philosophy was, "Let yourself go, express yourself, obey that impulse." We never asked if we had a self worth expressing. A distinguished American historian has called it the "dirty decade."

It is so today. High moral effort generated by the war is followed by a period of moral indifference. Just look around you today and see the flagrant violation of law, the vulgar indecencies of stage and screen, the inordinate display of wealth, dreadful juvenile delinquencies, and the increase in crimes of violence. Or look at this moral breakdown in its broader aspects. In the life of the nation there are signs of desperate moral instability. As I go up and down the country and listen to thoughtful people, I have discovered they do not ask, "Are we turning to the right of center, or are we turning to the left of center?" but, "Do we still have a center?" Many are wondering if there is still some moral beam by which we sail the course of the ship of state. These are days of expediency.

It is so easy to let "I will" wait upon "I would." We travel the primrose path of dalliance as individuals and nations. We have a way of pigeonholing an inconvenient conscience. We send up trial balloons to find out which way the wind is blowing before we express an opinion. Many gyrate from one side of the street to the other depending upon where the sun is shining. For the sake of applause or advantage we refuse to make up our minds. The preacher who would have a needed message for such an age must deal with that grim fact.

There is another interesting fact which cannot escape the discriminating observer. This is one of those inbetween periods of history. One world is passing away; another world is trying to be born. The angel with the flaming sword is standing at the gate to keep us from going back. We do not know where to go, but we are on the way. We are living in a kind of no man's land, far enough from each side to be counted out, but near enough to both to run for cover. The passage from light to light is through a zone of darkness or twilight. No one would doubt that much of the past is intolerable. There must come attitudes and patterns of life much more human and fair and just. But when one attitude of life is being supplanted by another approach to life, there is always fear and anxiety. The possibilities of failure, the uncertainty of success, the lack of experience, the fact that we have no precedent to guide us, fill us with misgivings and fear. So we both want it and don't want it; we both desire it and dread it; we seek it and yet we evade it. We do not know if change will be improvement. We are not so positive that a different world will be a better world.

In a way, of course, there is nothing new about living in a changing order. I recall one day visiting the Museum of Antiquity in Constantinople. There I saw under a glass case an old piece of papyrus, the oldest bit of writing paper known to man. What interested me was not so much the faded paper with its brittle edges, but the sentence that was written on it. It was this: "Alas times are not what they used to be; children no longer obey their parents and everybody is writing a book about it." You see, we have always lived in a changing world. New attitudes and values and patterns of life are seeking to express themselves. We live in a world which is at springtime. There will have to be a great deal of plowing and harrowing and sowing before the harvest appears. It requires not only courage but faith to live in such a day.

Let me suggest a third and obvious characteristic of our time. We are living for good or ill in a world with new and dangerous frontiers. There was a time when the boundaries of nations were determined by geography. The barriers which separated races and nations were natural barricades: a mountain range, a broad river, a wide sea, a belt of swamp land or forests. As long as these frontiers stood, nations thought themselves secure. No one from without could come in and no one from within could go out. Then came modern science and suddenly these natural barriers became meaningless and the frontiers of nations became imaginary lines. You can tunnel any hill, you can span a bridge across any river, you can sail any sea with a ship, and you can fly a plane over any hump. Indeed, there are not two places in the world more than 50 or 60 flying hours apart. You can fly around the whole world in 150 hours. You see, the normal frontiers of geography are meaningless.

34

Now in the attempt to protect themselves nations are building a new kind of frontier which is much more impenetrable and impregnable. These frontiers are not in the field of geography, but in the realm of the mind. They are invisible and sink very deep before you are aware of their existence. The new frontiers of nations are in reality the frontiers of suspicion, hate, fear, and power. Not long ago I asked a leader of the underground of one of the liberated countries of Europe what was the attitude of his country toward us. "Frankly," he said, "we do not like you." I replied, "But we have just finished fighting and dying for you." He replied, "That is true, but you are so very powerful; we do not know what you will do with us." So nations build the new frontiers of suspicion.

Let me give another illustration. I wonder if we are really aware of the fact that the atomic bomb has shaken the governments of the world to their very foundations. A very distinguished scientist said to me not long ago, "When I consider the moral level of the world of today, I am sorry we have made the discovery of atomic energy." It is a new frontier of fear. So one might multiply incident after incident. But there they are—dangerous frontiers. As long as these frontiers stand, we can never hope to achieve peace on earth. Believe me, it will take all the patience, all the forbearance, all the tolerance and all the grace of God we can possibly muster to live with reasonable contentment, and hold this world together. How can you preach without awareness of it?

The one unresolved problem of our time is, how can nations live together permanently and in peace? Is it possible to organize our world in such a way that men may return to their own tent doors with none to molest or make afraid or make ashamed? Can nations so adjust their differences that at the long last we may go on building a new heaven and a new earth? Is it possible for races and peoples to make such allowances for one another and to live with such a spirit of give-and-take that fear and frustration may pass away, and we may bring in, "peace on the earth, good will to men"?

Through the long centuries man has answered that question in part. We have learned to live together in units of family life. A group of people will live together under one roof. They are not of the same age, the same temper nor of the same taste. They do not dress alike, eat alike, or think alike. They do not have the same ambitions, the same attitudes, or the same perspectives. And yet, they are held together by that invisible bond of affection which over-rules all tension and strain. Then, too, we have learned to live together in units of community life. Until recently I had my home in a city where seven and one-half million people live together with reasonable decency, and in reasonable understanding. People have learned to adjust themselves to one another, put up with one another and make allowances for one another. The idea of the community has disciplined them in all their personal demands. That is partly true of nations. We have differing racial, religious, social, and ethnic backgrounds. But we have learned to live together for the common good, disciplining our individual desires and aspirations.

But beyond these, man has not yet learned to live in

good will and understanding with his fellow man. It is perhaps the most hazardous of our accomplishments. It is difficult business. Someone asked a war correspondent who had lived in London during those terrifying months when the city was blitzed what was the most trying part of the experience. He replied, "It was living in air-raid shelters night and day without privacy. People were always on top of one another all the time." Living together in a shrinking world brings complications and irritations.

The world may not yet be a brotherhood, but it is a neighborhood. This world is a whispering gallery. Sometimes an architect will build to scale a tiny replica of his project. There it is on the table, with streets and gardens and parks. The house is there, too, with the roof off so that you can look into every niche and corner and see what it is like everywhere. Well, we live in a world like that.

There is one respect in which our era is different from all other periods of human history. There is one thing which we no longer have which man has always had until this time. In the world of the past there were geographical frontiers. There were always areas undiscovered, and lands uninhabited. Man was always finding open spaces and islands and far-off lands where he could expand and develop. There was elbow room for all nations. People could expand without being pushed about. But now there are no geographical frontiers left. All the land that is on this earth is known and possessed and occupied. If nations expand from now on, it will have to be at the expense of other nations. When that happens, you have war. You see, we must do something about this problem of living together in good will because there is no land left.

The world has become too small. Since 1750, the beginning of the age of steam, the population of our earth has trebled. Before then periods when births were in excess of deaths alternated with periods when deaths were in excess of births. But the fact is that this world holds sixty-six per cent more people now than when the age of steam began. All this has come to pass in six generations. When you ask why that is, you discover it is because we have begun to depend upon one another. We live in a co-operative world whether we like it or not. Each nation produces goods and material, not simply for itself, but for the sake of people beyond the national frontiers. Nations are today keeping one another alive. It is actually true that we cannot live without one another.

But there is more to it than that. Not only is there no land left, but there is no time left. Always in the past we have been able to say, "Some day we will have to settle this issue, some day we will have to set up a technique of living together." But we could always push it off into the future. We would educate our children and let them grapple with the problem. Time was always on our side. We were content to leave it to our children or our children's children. But that is no longer possible. Time is no longer on our side. Time has run out on us. Suddenly the atomic bomb is loose in the universe. It is like a mine floating in steamship lanes. The world may blow up at any time. Man has now the capacity of destroying himself. We have actually invented tools for our own annihilation. Atomic energy is a force God has used to hold the universe together. We have learned one of the secrets of this energy. We have learned its exploding power. It is as if in an electric age the only thing we knew about electricity was how to electrocute people. This is one of those either-or times. There are tides in the affairs of men. It is either now or never. There is no longer any time left. One thinks of the laconic observation of the Duke of Wellington, "Nothing except a battle lost can be half so melancholy as a battle won." How can you preach to this generation without awareness of all that?

This is a world increasingly wrapped up in itself. People are becoming more and more absorbed in their own interests. Windows through which we were meant to look at the world have become mirrors. Ask the average G.I. in college what he wants, and he will tell you the one thing he wants is to settle down, have a home and family and children, have reasonable security, and then be left alone. All this self-absorption is creating strain and fear and frustration. H. G. Wells was reported to have said at the close of his last American tour, "American democracy breaks down five miles from the town pump." What he meant to say, of course, was that we are turning in on ourselves.

There is a word which we do not use often, for it is an ugly word, and it has such ugly connotations. It is the word "idiot." In reality it is a very good word which comes from the Greek *ideotes*, which means literally "private citizen." Just mull over that a little while, and you will do some sober thinking. To a life all wrapped up in itself everything ultimately becomes fantastic and idiotic. Political and religious isolationism do not make sense. Nations and peoples who become all wrapped up in themselves have no security or future.

Let me point to one more and perhaps the most significant characteristic of the age. No one with intelligence enough to know, or heart enough to care, or courage enough to face the facts can possibly doubt that a poignant sense of wistfulness is surging through the world. In the heart of our generation there is a nameless, ageless, indefinable longing for something, men know not what, but without which they will never know joy nor peace nor strength. Man's search for God is on. Our generation may disavow that fact and keep talking about the quest for reality and security, but they all come to the same thing. A man may have a garage full of cars, a bank full of money, a house full of children, a library full of books and a museum full of pictures, but scratch the surface, and you will come upon an appalling emptiness. Believe me, behind the iron curtain of fear and frustration is a longing for God.

Life still is today as John Bunyan saw it three centuries ago: a man in filthy rags, with a scroll under his arm, with his back upon his home, in the City of Destruction, looking for the gateway of the Interpreter. We seem like people who walk on streets which have no foundation. We seem like boats on muddy flats with never a white sail in sight. We seem like sleepers, conscious of the dawn, but unable to awaken. In the heart of our generation there is a search for a depth so deep, a height so inaccessible, a distance so long that nothing can reach it or touch it. What we supposed was an oasis has proven to be a mirage. What we thought were palm trees are only scarred rocks standing on the edge of barren desert sands.

Not long ago a very cultured and cultivated young woman came to see me. She wanted to know something about religion, and more specifically about the Christian faith. After talking with her for a long time I said to her, "How did you get this way? What led you to come here for this?" Then she told me that she had at home a seventeen-weeks-old baby. She didn't want that little child to miss something which she had missed, and she believed it was God. Our prodigal world has come to that bend in the road when the angel of its better self calls out, "I will arise and go to my father."

There are so many evidences of this wistfulness which are all too familiar to those who deal with the day-by-day people. All manner of cults are growing up around us like mushrooms, to which people turn only to fall back in the end, disillusioned. The land is full of what Dr. Paul Scherer called "swamis with and without turbans," trying to tell people how and where to find peace. They are blind leaders of the blind saying, "Lo, here, lo, there." Our world today is full of isms and wasms. You may laugh at them, but there they are—symptoms of an inner urge, pitiful expressions of an indefinable longing. John Burroughs seemed to speak for them when he wrote in one of his last essays, "I wish someone would light up the way for me."

People know that science can air condition houses. But science can never turn a house into a home. Only God can do that. Science can go to the laboratory and make penicillin for the healing of the body; but science cannot minister to a mind diseased or pluck from the memory a rooted sorrow. Only God can do that. Science can rebuild the bombed cities of Europe and Asia; but science cannot rebuild the blasted lives of a shattered world. Only God can do that. Science can put into man's hand the atomic bomb by which he can destroy himself; but science can't resolve the problems which the atomic bomb creates. Only God can do that. Science has been able to lengthen human life, breed faster horses, dig deeper tunnels, build taller buildings and construct longer bridges; science has enabled man to fly into the stratosphere and to descend into the very bowels of the sea.

But science has also brought sweat shops, ghettos, industrial discontent, concentration camps, and share croppers. It has brought moral sterility, emotional instability, mental boredom, and spiritual insensitiveness. It has brought into being what Carlyle said would come: The universe has become a vast juggernaut tearing man limb from limb.

In circuses and carnivals you will often come upon a side show known as the "hall of mirrors." You stand before one and you become a tall, thin, cadaverous bean-pole sort of person. Stand before another and you become a pudgy, squatty, barrel-figured Santa Claus. But walk back into the open and you are still the same kind of person. So it is with man. For all his genius, abnormality, and grotesque proportions, he is still the same, and longs for something better beyond himself. The fashionable skepticism with which education has veneered us has brought man to the attitude of despair. Varnish always melts under heat. Man's self-confidence based upon Herbert Spencer's philosophy of the inevitability of progress has been utterly shattered.

Some years ago a friend of mine, a distinguished educator, was visiting Rome with his wife. Late one afternoon they went to St. Peter's. They walked leisurely through the long nave until they came to the high altar. They stood facing it with a sense of reverence. His wife wandered away to examine something which interested her. The educator turned around and stood with his back to the altar to take in the vast cathedral. Now it happened that many devout people were walking through the church, plain people, nuns, and priests. As they approached the altar, they bowed solemnly and in great dignity. The educator supposed they were curtsying to him so he bowed in turn to them. This went on for some time until his wife saw it, walked rapidly to him, and giving a tug at his sleeve, said, "You are suffering from an omnipotence complex." How much of that one sees today. So many will take the bows and curtain calls for Deity, arrogate to themselves a final judgment upon everything, until they even fashion God after their own likeness.

You come upon that in the world of culture. For more than a generation there has been a constant emphasis on the importance of knowledge. We thought of it as an end in itself. We had come to believe that, if we only knew enough, then a better world would come. We should have known better, for the Greeks tried that and failed. We know enough—indeed, we are too clever for our own good —but we are not good enough. All this has led to smugness

43

and sophistication. We have come to believe that man is great in proportion as the sense of mystery vanishes. We supposed that the absence of faith was a sign of intellectual acumen when, as a matter of fact, it is the inevitable earmark of a second-rate civilization. Theodore Roosevelt never spoke more profoundly: "To train a man mentally without training him morally and spiritually is to make him a menace to society."

One comes upon this also in the realm of government. The purpose of government is to provide a technique whereby people in a given area or country can live together in happiness, contentment, and security. Government is in reality an instrument of progress, a means of achieving a common goal and a common good. But today government is no longer a means but an end. We are witnessing today the birth of statism in many forms. It demands man's unquestioning loyalty of body, mind, and soul. There is no such thing as conscience apart from the interests of the state. The means have become ends, and we have made a god of government. There have been four factors in the making of a nation: home, church, school, and state. Hitherto the first three have always been the most important, and the last, least important. Today what is the least important has arrogated to itself the rights of the most important. What is most important has abrogated and capitulated to what is the least important. If I might paraphrase an ancient psalm, modern man has come to say, "The State is my shepherd; I shall not want. It leadeth me beside the still waters; it restoreth my soul."

But all this has not turned out very well. One thinks

of the poignant comment which Max Muller made years after he had been made a member of the French Academy of Science, which honor he longed for: "The dream of reality was greater than the reality of the dream."

To see the world after this fashion is not an invitation to despair. The very wistfulness of the times has in it an element of hope. This is no time for puling and wailing. If the things that are wrong did not tumble apart every now and again, if evil were not visited with some kind of stern judgment, and if the wrong always went unchallenged, then I would lose my faith. On that basis, life would become insanity and the world a madhouse. The very tumbling apart of so much that we thought was permanent is a challenge to faith. Indeed, these times have not slackened my belief in God, but have strengthened it. It is our business to take the things that still remain and build on them a braver and better tomorrow.

You will recall that long-ago day of the divided kingdom. The ancient Hebrew people had fallen apart into two brittle groups. There was the kingdom of the north with ten tribes and the kingdom of the south with two tribes. The kingdom of the north, which was much stronger, made an attack upon the kingdom of the south and threw a blockade against its frontiers, hoping to starve it to death or surrender. They built a huge Siegfried Line, anchored on the city of Ramah, which they crowded with troops and the munitions of war. The king of the south knew he was doomed; so he resorted to a clever bit of strategy. He made a treaty with the king of Syria, whose lands bordered on the northern frontiers of the northern kingdom. In accordance with this treaty the king of Syria made an attack upon the kingdom of the north and so relieved the pressure upon the much smaller armies of the kingdom of the south.

The strategy was successful beyond words. The northern kingdom had to abandon its frontiers at Ramah to protect its own lines. At once the king of Judah attacked from the south and had no difficulty in utterly destroying the blockade and reducing it to rubble. But the king of Judah was not only a good strategist, but also a good psychologist. He knew that as long as these bits of stone and rubble were left they would only breed a determination on the part of the northern kingdom to wreak revenge and rebuild that broken line. So we read, "They carried away the stones of Ramah and the timbers thereof . . . ; and he built therewith . . . Mizpah." The very elements which would breed revenge he used in the reconstruction of the city of peace.

That is our business in the world. Out of the wreckage and rubble of a broken world, the existence of which in themselves constitutes elements of danger, we are to build the kingdom of heaven. So shall we stand before God and this age unashamed and unafraid.

III. These Things Have Been Written

I BELONG TO THOSE FORTUNATE GROUPS OF PEOPLE WHO were brought up on the Bible. In the formative years of my life I never lived beyond the sight and sound of that Book. In my boyhood home after each meal some sentences were read out of it. On Sunday evenings at twilight time as the shadows lengthened my father would gather us together, and we would sing the Sabbath hymns of our faith, after which my father would read to us out of the Book and expound it. The psalmody of David, the matchless fifty-fifth chapter of Isaiah, the incomparable parables of Jesus, the unforgettable stories of Providence, the love story of Ruth, the visions of the prophets and the apocalypse of John were part of my day-by-day life. "Come unto me all ye that labor," "God so loved the world that he gave his only begotten Son," "The Lord is my shepherd, I shall not want," "By grace are ye saved through faith," "If with all your hearts ye truly seek me,"—these were household sentences in the home of my childhood.

I do not recall all that as a depressing experience. I felt at that time no sense of hardship or severity or resentment toward it. Indeed, I thought myself a fortunate boy growing up in that kind of a home, and I look back upon it now as a blessed heritage. I would rather have the memory of those experiences than all the bags of gold you can drag through Wall Street.

Then, too, I was brought up to believe that the Bible is the source book of all that is best in culture, philosophy, and wisdom. Bach and Beethoven, Haydn and Händel were steeped in its truth. Reubens and Raphael, Titian and Tintoretto, Watts and Hoffman turned to it for their themes. Milton, Dante, Tennyson, Browning, and Bunyan found in it their inspiration. Webster, Pitt, and Burke gained persuasive powers and oratorical abilities because of their familiarity with the laws of Moses and the prophet Isaiah. All the great of earth from Paul to Lincoln have gone forth as knights-errant upon their crusades of right-eousness and compassion with their "feet shod with the preparation of the gospel." Countries where democracy has made its greatest impact have always had the open Book, known and read by all people.

I was also brought up to believe that the language of the Bible had entered into our day-by-day life. A knowl-edge of the Bible would enlarge and enrich my vocabulary. There are certain phrases and sentences current in our daily speech which have no meaning apart from that Book. We speak of the "salt of the earth," "a mess of pottage," "a labor of love," "the valley of decision," "a drop in the bucket," "apple of the eye," "a wolf in sheep's clothing," "a house divided against itself," "sweeter than honey," "clear as crystal," "wise as serpents." What are these but tiny phrases out of the Book? They have no meaning apart from the Book. You see, I was brought up to know and revere the Book.

But as I grew up, there came to me a depressing sense of disillusionment. I had supposed that what I had been brought up to believe was a matter of universal acceptance. Often I found myself among those who discredited the Book. Apparently something had happened to it, in the light of scientific investigation and historical research, so that I could no longer believe it to be the Book it was when I read it at my mother's knee. The arguments which led many to disavow this Book were not always clear, but there seemed to be a growing opinion that something had happened to it which it could never recover. Of course, as time went on I discovered that this historical research did not in any way discredit the Book, but rather strengthened its claim. The more it was studied, the deeper became the conviction of its genuineness. It stood the test of criticism and research. It was still the Word of God and always has been to me. The first question it asks is not, "Is it beautiful?" but "Is it true?"

Then, too, I discovered not only that in some circles the Bible was discredited and disavowed, but what is worse, it was disregarded. People just brushed it aside. It was thought of as a collection of saga and folklore with no particular bearing on our times. H. G. Wells said one day, "The Book is out of date. It ought to be brought up to date." Indeed, it was a sign of intellectual superiority to push it aside. Those who read it were low-brow. It had a place in the day of the tallow candle and horse-and-buggy, but so much in it was unscientific and fantastic that it was not even good taste to be found reading it. The Book was not read. The free public-school system of this country was initiated in Massachusetts in order that the children might grow up to know the Bible. Now in the average public school they read almost every other book except the Bible. In such homes as there is still place for it, it is often used as a doorstop or paper weight. It became a convenient thing upon which to take an oath before the court.

Of course, we paid dearly for all that. A civilization which disavows "thus saith the Lord," has no future and no security. Those who put the Book out of their lives soon discovered that they were walking on streets that had no foundations and eating food which did not nourish. There was left to them no lee of shore to which they could run in time of storm. There was no rock upon which they could plant their feet. There was no anchor they could cast in the face of driving winds.

But we have struck bottom on all that now. With the resurgence of interest in the Bible there is always a peril. We turned to it in the days of darkness and dilemma and found it a help in the blistering emergency of war. It is quite possible that when the emergency passes there will pass with it this appreciation and reverence for the Book. What is, therefore, needed today is that we shall make the Bible meaningful to people in their day-by-day lives. How can we do that? Out of my own personal experience in counseling I am convinced that there are three facts about the Bible which will make the Book meaningful to people, and make of it something more than a fetish.

The Bible will become meaningful when people remember that it is not a book but a library. It is made up of sixty-six different books—thirty-nine in the Old Testament and twenty-seven in the New Testament. It was not written at one sitting and so tossed off into history. Mark Twain once said that "a Bible like that would be chloroform in print." The Bible was written by some forty people over a period of time of fifteen hundred years in an area equivalent to that which lies between the Atlantic seaboard and the Rocky Mountains. It was written by different kinds of people. Among these writers there was a shepherd, a physician, a king, a farmer, a historian, a poet, a fisherman, a priest, a lawyer, and a philosopher. It was written by different men with different backgrounds facing different needs and different dilemmas. Each tried to meet some one problem that was foremost in the minds of the people for whom he wrote. Each wrote independently of the other. You have, therefore, in the Bible two thousand years of changing life; yet the Book does not change.

Because it was written by so many different kinds of people it is at home in the cottage and in the palace, in the courthouse and in the prison; in hospitals and in fox holes; in cathedrals and at firesides. When people read the Bible they should go to it as they go to a library. Sometimes they will be in the mood for poetry; then they turn to the Psalms. Sometimes they feel in the mood for romance, and they will come upon the incomparable love story of Ruth. Sometimes they are historically minded, and then the books of Judges and of the Kings open before them. Sometimes they feel the need of some quickening impact upon the conscience; then the books of the law become most helpful. There are times when they wonder what life and the universe are all about; then it is that the sense of purpose and the destiny of life will be clarified in the rich imagery and revelations of the prophets and of the Apostle John. When people use the Bible in some such fashion, they will never become wearied of it, but will have a longing for it.

The Bible will become meaningful when people use it as a source book of aspiration. The Bible is like a winding road up which humanity travels to the home of the soul. It is a record of man's ageless, nameless, indefinable longing for something, he knows not what, but without which, he will never know peace or joy. It is the unending story of prodigal humanity saying, "I will arise and go to my father." Through this Book man approaches God through prayer, sacrifice, faith, dreams, and worship. Here you have man's ageless search for God.

Among the Sioux Indians it was a custom that when a boy became twelve years of age and entered his adolescence, the chiefs of the tribe would give him a series of instructions. He was ordered to leave the camp and live for three days in the wilderness. He was given a bow and arrow but was ordered not to kill because he was to learn the lesson of discipline. Every evening at twilight he was ordered to climb a certain hill near the camp, and there silhouetted against a dying sun was ordered to pray, "Here, God, poor and needy I stand." That is the lesson of the Bible to all times.

If people want to know what lies at the center of it,

52

they must go back to read, "As the hart panteth after the water brooks, so panteth my soul after thee, O God." In adoration it sings, "I was glad when they said unto me, let us go into the house of the Lord." In times of wistfulness the Book lifts the poignant call, "Oh that I knew where I might find him!" In hours of penitence it calls out, "Create in me a clean heart, O God."

You will meet people in this Book who have the same hopes and aspirations, the same dilemmas and disillusionments which surge through you. Modern anxieties, uncertainties, and misgivings they experienced too. The difficulties and the blasted hopes which are so commonplace in life today they knew all about. If people want to know how to meet life in times like that, they can go back to find how men and women long ago met life in those same settings. If people will read the Bible as a source book of aspiration, they will never permit the dust to collect on the cover.

But most of all the Bible will become meaningful when people use it as a source book of assurance. It is not enough that man shall reach up his hand to heaven for help; what he wants to know is if there is somewhere a hand that reaches down to him. The Bible never leaves you long in the dark about that. It is not only the story of the search of man for God, but also the search of God for man. It is a highway on which man travels through prayer, fasts, and sacrifices. But it is a two-way street. It is also a highway down which God travels to man through revelations, providences, assurances, and laws. The Bible is a book about God.

53

Indeed, it is a rather unscientific book. I, for one, am glad it is so. If it were a scientific book, it would have to be altered every ten years. It is not a book about science, although it has much scientific data. It is not a book about botany, although it has a great deal to say about flowers. It is not a book on astronomy, although it has some lovely things to tell us about the stars. It is not a book of jurisprudence, although law is there. If you want to know what stands at the center of it you must read again, "And ye shall seek me, and find me, when ye shall search for me with all your heart." The Bible does not tell us how to make machinery, but it does tell us how to make men who are safe with machines. It does not give us political techniques, but it does tell us how to make men who can be trusted with government. It does not tell us how to build roads, but it does tell us how to make men who can be trusted on these roads. It is a book about God. It gives courage to the timid, companionship to the lonely, confidence to the confused, and forgiveness to the sinful.

But someone will say, "How can an infinite God make himself known to finite man? Is it possible for finite man to interpret an infinite God? What assurance have we that man can grasp the idea of God? How can the finite grasp the infinite?" Well, I think there are two simple answers. The first is this: One day you go to your victrola to play an old favorite song of some great artist. You haven't heard that song for a long time, nor have you used the victrola. You discover that the needle is poor, that the connections are loose, that the record is warped. And yet you recognize the voice; it is unmistakable, there it is. So it is in this Book.

For all his failings and shortcomings man, made in the image of God, has been able to understand him and say with Kepler, "I think Thy thoughts after Thee, O God." There have been men through the long centuries who have walked so close to God and have been lifted so near to him that they saw what nobody else saw, heard what nobody else heard, felt what nobody else felt. What they heard, saw, and felt they wrote down and transmitted to the ages.

But there is a second answer. It is true that there are ideas too big for words. Language breaks down in the attempt to describe the infinite. You can never petrify timeless truth into the fixed forms of words. Then it is that the New Testament opens and you come face to face with the Word that becomes flesh. Jesus Christ is the Word of God. What he was in the days of his flesh God is throughout all ages. In Christ God is revealed. Indeed, he is God incarnate.

The Bible offers the assurance that God will see us through. It opens with the message, "Let there be light," and closes with the assurance, "Let there be life." It begins with a morning that ends with the evening. It concludes with an evening that ends in morning. It opens with the story of a shut gate and closes with the story of an open door. It begins with an angel with a flaming sword, and it ends with the story of a bride. It opens with condemnation; it ends with an invitation. David said to Saul:

> "Thou shalt love and be loved by, forever: a Hand like this hand
> Shall throw open the gates of new life to thee! See the Christ stand!"

The Book opens with the fashioning of the earth: the moon, star clusters, trees, skies, milky ways, apple blossoms. It records the beginning of man, of the family, of the tribe, of the nation. It tells by what laws man must live if he is to have peace and happiness: the social laws, political disciplines, economic regulations. It points to prayers and homilies which will enable men to keep these laws. You will meet the prophets who open new vistas of glory.

Then the road bends and you meet the Word of God incarnate, and hear the testimony of his followers. There follow the founding of the Church, the odyssey of its conquests, and the guiding letters of the apostles. It concludes with the apocalypse of John upon the beetling cliffs of Patmos, shouting across the tumbling centuries, "Hallelujah: for the Lord God omnipotent reigneth."

> It wakes desires you never may forget,
> It shows you stars you never saw before,
> It makes you share with Him forever more
> The burden of the world's divine regret.

It is never out of date. It never grows old. Go to your library and the books current ten years ago make dull reading. Nothing is so insipid as yesterday's newspaper. Carlyle called it "a bit of rag with print on it." But not so the Book. Grass grows and withers, leaving the problem of hunger unsolved. Rain falls, but clouds vanish leaving thirst unslaked. Flowers bloom and fade leaving the longing for beauty unsatisfied. But the Word of God endures forever, and satisfies.

One day three men were sitting in a reading room in the British Museum. It was lunch hour. Two of the men were nibbling a sandwich. Some distance from them sat the third. The two men were making fun of "that German with more than a touch of Jerusalem" reading day after day the philosophy of Hegel and making voluminous notes. They called him the dreamer and spinner of cobwebs. But the name of that spinner of cobwebs was Karl Marx. His broodings in the museum reading room have shaken the world. But we have a book within our reach infinitely richer, deeper, and more explosive, making available the power of God in day-by-day life. It provides life with a rock no storm can beat down. It is a hand which no panic can shorten. It offers a light which no darkness can dim. Would that people would begin to read it afresh.

I shall never forget the day when I held in my hands for the first time the Bible of Abraham Lincoln. It was the only book he carried with him out of Nolin Creek, Pigeon Creek, and the Sangamon to the Potomac. Strangely enough, the book fell open in my lap to the thirty-seventh psalm. He must have read it many times for the page was thumb-marked. "Fret not thyself because of evil doers. . . . Rest in the Lord, and wait patiently for him. . . . and he shall give thee the desires of thine heart." One day, speaking of the Bible, Lincoln gave the good advice, "Accept all you can by reason and the rest by faith, and you will live and die a better man." The Book will lift horizons, push back foot-hills, resolve tensions and clarify many things that seem obscure.

While no one would doubt the importance of the Bible in the day-by-day lives of people, let it be said at once that it must become even more important in the day-by-day life of the preacher. However much we vary in our interpretation, with whatever differing attitudes we may approach it, not many would doubt that the preacher who is to stand up unashamed and unafraid must know his Book. It is his treasure-trove. It abounds in illustrations and figures of speech and symbols. It holds the rarest poetry that has ever been written and the profoundest philosophy that men have ever thought through. It is full of material which is grist in the mill of the preacher.

However critical we may be of a generation which is growing up unfamiliar with the Bible, the simple fact is that it is nobody's fault but our own. There has been too much preaching on current events, contemporary issues, and what the Germans called the "zeitgeist," utterly disassociated from any contact with the Bible. Too much preaching has separated itself from the Book. We seem to make more of the quotations of contemporary thinkers than the writers of the ancient Book. Indeed, it is no longer in vogue even to have a text.

It is true there is an appalling ignorance of the Book on the part of the laity, but as I go up and down I discover an even greater ignorance of the Book on the part of too many of the clergy. For one reason or another in too many instances it is brushed aside. Too many have been cowed by this quasi-intellectual criticism which looks down its nose at the Book. One wonders if we are not ourselves responsible for the fact that the Bible is not known or understood. We are afraid that when preaching becomes Bible-centered it will cease to be popular and attractive. What needs to be said to the ministry today is, "Go back to the Book and stay there."

After all, it is the Word of God. It is, of course, the source book of much material that goes into the building of the sermon, but there is more to it than that. In this Book God has spoken to the ages, and we are his ambassadors. It is our business to see that his utterances and words shall be given to the age. It may be that in the past too much was claimed for the Bible, but you do not solve that problem by making nothing of it. I am reminded of a sentence which Dr. John Watson, more familiarly known as Ian Maclaren, wrote in one of his lectures which an untimely death prevented him from delivering. "Our forefathers were too sure of everything, but it would be a good thing if we became sure of some things." The preacher who goes back to the Book has behind him an authority which is not of man.

I recall one day meeting with a group of students at a New England university. They wanted to discuss the value of religion. Now I have lived long enough to know that debating religion with any man accomplishes little good. At the end of the debate each side is apt to go back with his prejudices confirmed. So I said to them, "Suppose I tell you what I believe; then you can tell the group what you believe, and you can make your choice." They asked me to begin, and I did. Before I got half through one of the students sitting directly in front of me half-rose out of his chair, pointed his finger at me, and said somewhat cynically, "Well, that is what you think." And of course the boy was right. If what I discussed at that moment was a matter of opinion with me, it had no more significance than the opinion of anyone else. But when I told him that I was simply quoting from the New Testament from which I had my authority, he had no answer. Most people don't care what we think. They want to know what God says. You will preach with greater confidence and with greater helpfulness to people when you anchor what you say upon what God has said.

And that Book lends itself to preaching. If we could read the Bible with imagination and insight, it would become more vibrant with new meaning. The more you read it, the deeper you ponder it, the more relevant does it become.

Shortly before the explosion of the atomic bomb at Bikini a very distinguished New York newspaperman came to see me. He wanted to know if the Bible had anything to say about atomic bombs. After some discussion I read to him that amazing sentence in II Pet. 3:10-11:

But the day of the Lord will come as a thief in the night; in the which the heavens shall pass away with a great noise, and the elements shall melt with fervent heat, the earth also and the works that are therein shall be burned up. Seeing then that all these things shall be dissolved, what manner of persons ought ye to be.

He seemed rather startled and said, "I have before me the confidential reports which have been released with reference to the atomic-bomb experiment." He said the scientist who wrote the report used almost the same words which were found in the New Testament. You see, the Bible is not as outworn or outmoded as men sometimes think. It has a profound relevance for contemporary life.

For many years, indeed as long as I was the minister of a parish church, I observed a custom which became a sort of ritual with me. In the summertime when we go to the country, I rise rather early and sit alone either in the morning sun or before the fireplace with my King James version. I also have with me the translations of Moffatt, Weymouth, and Goodspeed. I then begin by selecting some book. I read very slowly and creatively until some word or text strikes me full in the face. Then I stop my reading and put it down in a loose-leaf notebook at my side. It may be a word or an idea which has suggested itself in some fashion. I put down every thought which comes to me in that quiet period of reading. If during the day this idea unfolds, I put it down before the day is over. The next morning I begin reading where I left off and follow the same procedure. By the end of the summer I have, therefore, ample material on which I can creatively work and use as my backlog for months to come. I keep on working in this loose-leaf notebook constantly.

Let me illustrate what I mean. No one can question the sense of disillusionment which surges through our times. A strange cynicism is gnawing at the lute-strings of life. People have come to believe that all life will fade into oblivion. When I tried to deal with that issue and what the Bible had to say about it, I came one day in my reading upon this sentence in Genesis: "And the evening and the

morning were the first day." I would not have written it
like that. It seemed like a clerical error. Most of us would
have written it: "And the morning and the evening were the
first day." But it is not so in the Book. Lest you think it was
a clerical error, for your benefit it is repeated five times.
What does it mean? Simply this: God's day always ends in
dawn. There is no finality about darkness and shadows. It
is rather suggestive that in the last book of the Bible you
read, "There shall be no night." What incontestable evidence you have here of the ultimate triumph of the pur-
poses of God.

Take another instance. Most of us are greatly disturbed
about the emphasis upon externals in present-day living.
We seem to be less and less concerned about the things that
lie at the center. Every minister knows that he faces the
appalling secularization of life. If you make a frontal attack on that sort of thing, you often arouse needless op-
position. So it was that one day I fell to reading the moving
story of Abraham and his little lad Isaac going on a retreat,
hoping for a fresh experience of God's presence. They go
trudging up the hill, until at last, after all preparation has
been made, Isaac says to his father, "Behold the wood and
the fire but where is the lamb?" Are there not many asking
that question today?

Sometimes we wonder why the Bible is cluttered up with
so many regulations, customs, and practices which may
have significance for the historian or antiquarian but have
seemingly no value for life today. Well, let us see. The book
of Leviticus is full of these statutes and regulations. There
was a law that in reaping, the grain which could not be

taken in the first cutting was to be left for the poor and the needy. The law was, "Thou shalt not wholly reap the corners of thy field." If modern man could walk around that regulation a little while, most of the every-day problems would soon be resolved; because it simply means that man is not entitled to everything he can put his hands on.

Take another emphasis. Much is being made of confessions of faith. We are very vocal about them, but we are not so very vocal about confessions of sin. I recall making a study of the number of instances in which man made a confession of sin. I found seven in all, beginning with the confession of Pharaoh, "I have sinned this time. . . . I and my people are very wicked." The last is the confession of Judas, "I have sinned in that I have betrayed the innocent blood." In these seven confessions of the Book you will find the whole sweep of the tragedy and frightening consequences of evil in every age. Believe me, they need to be made today.

I commend to you a study of Christ as he stands revealed in the Old Testament. The Old Testament abounds in many and varying symbols and figures of speech used to describe his character. Long before he walked this earth, men with the souls of poets and vision of seers saw him come and described what manner of man he would be. They spoke of him as "a root out of dry ground." Some called him the "lily of the valley." They said he would be the "Prince of Peace." They called him a "lion of the tribe of Judah." They said he would be a "suffering servant." The last figure of speech used to describe him is that which called him "the dawn." They said, "He shall feed his flock like a shepherd." You can make Christ live for people if you can make the Book live in your own thinking and preaching.

What is needed today is that the preacher and the teacher read this Book with imagination until there stand illuminated sentences such as: "And the angel said unto him, . . . bind on thy sandals"; "John did no miracles"; "Thou hast nothing to draw with, and the well is deep"; "They took him even as he was, . . . and there arose a great storm." One could go on. If people do not know the Bible and do not know how to read it, the minister and teacher have a duty to make that Book live. It is expository preaching which the age needs, if it is to be rooted and grounded in truth.

I suppose every minister has some sentence of the Book which, through the years, has become the anchor of his soul. I have such a golden text. Years ago I was passing through a very disillusioning experience which left me bewildered. Then one day quite casually I opened my Bible, and my eyes fell upon the sentence which has forever changed me. It was the sentence of Jesus in John 8:29, "He that sent me is with me. The Father hath not left me alone." From that hour everything in life has been different. Not a day has passed since then but what I have repeated it to myself, and many who have come to me for counsel have heard me urge this sentence upon them. It has turned the tide of life for many people under many varying circumstances.

The morning when my eyes fell upon it I learned two

things which I have never forgotten. The first is that there rests upon life a sense of divine mission. Through every episode and incident there runs a divine purpose. We are not bits of flotsam or jetsam cast by the tides of time upon the shores of a relentless fate. It may not be a pleasant mission upon which we are sent, but we cannot walk out on it. God did not send us into this world to debate that mission but to fulfill it. With that simple fact there comes another: "The Father hath not left me alone." We do not make our way alone through the world. When you begin to falter, God does not bow himself out of life. When the lamps of reason flicker and the lights go out, then over the broken waves of life comes the final assurance, "Lo, I am with you alway, even to the end of the world." By these two convictions which I found in this golden text, I have lived my life. You are not alone; the centuries fight for you; eternity is your ally; you are in the keeping of one who holds you with love that will not let you go.

To every minister of religion and teacher this Book is indeed a "lamp unto my feet and a light unto my path." Saturate your language with its vocabulary; your mind with its truth; your heart with its love; your conscience with its laws; and your life with its spirit. It will lift horizons, push back foothills, and you will preach unashamed and unafraid.

IV. Reconciling the World Unto Himself

IT IS QUITE GENERALLY AGREED THERE MUST COME THREE emphases to modern preaching. In the world of tomorrow these three will have increasing importance and must be in the forefront of all planning. No preacher can stand before his generation unashamed and unafraid unless he is solemnly aware of them.

First, there must come a new emphasis upon ecumenical religion. The word ecumenical is much to the fore. Sometimes I think if we had another word for it, there would be more of it. It is an attempt to clarify the sense and consciousness of oneness in the Christian Church. Then, too, there must come an increasing emphasis on personal religion. There is too much professionalism in the ministry of today. Too often it does not go far beyond a formal approval. Many have concluded to give intellectual assent to the requirements of the Church is all that is required of them. What you say about religion must conform to the way you live with religion.

But there is a third needed emphasis in modern preaching. We need the emphasis, now forgotten, on doctrine. There is an appalling ignorance of the faith which we profess. Indeed, many have come to believe that the Christian discipleship is not founded upon any deep or lasting conviction. We are thought of as a company of pious well-wishers who really do not know what it is all about, mere busybodies running about furiously upon this or that crusade. We seemingly have forgotten that it is possible to become all things to all men until in the end you become nothing to any man. We need to hear again the admonition of Peter to the early Church, "Be ready always to give an answer to every man that asketh a reason of the hope that is in you." After all, we are ambassadors whose main business it is to make clear and compelling who and what we represent.

There is a great longing and desire on the part of people to know what is this faith once and for all delivered unto the saints. People turn to religion for three things. Throughout all ages and in all lands men have turned their faces to God for light, for comfort, and for courage. There are the seekers after truth, lonely souls in the vanguard of faith carrying their little lamps into impenetrable darkness, asking in the words of Bunyan, for the gateway of the Interpreter. They turn to God for light.

There are others who turn to religion for comfort. Perhaps a desperate sin has left them with a sense of guilt. Perhaps some cruel blow has fallen upon them, and they wonder if there is a balm in Gilead. For them hope no longer sees a star, the lamps are going out, and the lights are flickering. They turn to God for comfort.

But there are other times when men turn to him for courage. They find themselves bewildered and frustrated. The designs and machinations of men are too much for them. They are unequal to the battle. They wonder how they can keep going on and on and not fail. They want courage. They wonder whether Christianity can make good its claim. They do not question its genuineness but only question its relevance and meaning for life today. In other words they want to know what is the central message of the Christian faith.

Many times of late I have been asking myself what it was that Jesus was constantly preaching about? What was the one great theme, the constant refrain which ran through his ministry? It is possible to know what that was. I suppose that the Gospel of Mark is nearer to the life and ministry of Jesus than any other Gospel. Indeed, it is quite possible to suppose it became the source book of the Gospels written afterward. One can well imagine as Peter came to the end of his day, that Mark, his amanuensis, must have asked this same question, "What was Jesus always preaching about?" As Peter sat back and ran his fingers over the threads of memory and recalled these days he replied, "Jesus came into Galilee preaching the gospel of the kingdom of God." There you have it. In the Magna Charta of the Christian faith, commonly called the Sermon on the Mount, this was the constant emphasis.

He was always talking about God. It was knowing God and seeing God and being like God which was the burden of his message. He bore witness to it in his own life. As a boy of twelve you hear him say, "I must be about my Father's business." He came to the mature years saying, "I have meat to eat that ye know not of. . . . My meat is to do the will of him that sent me." In the end of the end he

68

climbed his Calvary, and you hear him say, "Father, into thy hands I commend my spirit." Whatever men may or may not believe about him, they are agreed that he lived with a God-consciousness. He did not tell men what to do or what not to do, but he gave them a new quality of life—a God-awareness.

That was the central message in the preaching of the disciples. They went everywhere bearing witness to Jesus' way of life—putting God in the center. They had no program, offered no Eldorado, built no utopia, and printed no blueprints. And yet a broken world they mended, political disintegration gave way to unity and economic injustice was resolved in contentment. The assurance of the love of God gave them a new enthusiasm for righteousness, a new love for their fellow men, a new understanding of need.

Always through history the Christian Church has held fast to that central conviction. The true herald of Christ is not a kind of man who stands first on one foot, then on the other, with his tongue in his cheek, mumbling something about not being sure of himself, apologizing for everything that is omnipotent in God, divine in Christ, and miraculous in his kingdom. The worthy apostle stands firmly on a rock which no storm can beat down. He never accommodates himself to the pressure groups of contemporary thought. He carries the light no darkness can dim. The minister who has no deep convictions and affirmations to which he conditions all he says and does, who adjusts his message to every whim, never sure of his footing, yielding here and giving ground somewhere else, is like a man who, having dug a hole, is forced to dig another in order to get rid of the earth which he has taken out of the first hole, and then must dig a third hole to get rid of the earth which he has taken out of the second hole and so, ad infinitum. Vagueness often ends in vacancy. The glib and fashionable skepticism with which education has veneered us has no place in him. An ambassador to a foreign court must be familiar with the laws, practices, political philosophy, history, and people of the country he represents. So the Christian minister.

What is the central conviction? You can read it in the classic sentence of Paul, "God was in Christ, reconciling the world unto himself." It is the conviction that a God of love stands in the center of the universe. It is the belief that what holds the world together is not chemistry but spirituality, not blind chance but eternal purpose.

It is a significant fact that the Christian religion turns on four great days, and these four great days are founded upon four great convictions. There is Christmas Day, Good Friday, Easter Day and the Day of Pentecost. They bear witness to historic facts: the birth of Christ, the atoning sacrifice upon the cross, the Resurrection, and the outpouring of the Holy Spirit. In the first you have God incarnate; in the second you have God redeeming; in the third you have God triumphing; and in the fourth you have God eternally present. To all these the Christian Church has borne witness in a common confession of faith which it has repeated in unison for sixteen hundred years, "I believe in God the Father Almighty."

This conviction alone can redeem mankind from secularism, which puts possession above purpose; from racialism, which denies the oneness of man in God; from scientism, which concerns itself with motion but not direction; from intellectualism, which smugly disavows what is beyond understanding; and from existentialism, which sees nothing beyond despair. Whenever the Christian Church has held fast to this central message, it has been strong. When it has failed to proclaim it, the Church has always become weak and compromising.

Early in the war I was speaking at an Army camp on the Atlantic seaboard. Late that first night I was walking with a soldier to the edge of the camp. When we arrived there, the sirens began to scream, and the lights in the camp went out. Suddenly from the hills all around the camp searchlights were turned on, trying to catch a plane which was coming in from over the Atlantic. Of course it proved to be an experimental flight, but in that hour no one knew what it might be. It was an awesome sight as one of these beams caught this plane until it seemed to hang silhouetted in the night sky. The soldier with me was obviously disturbed and said to me, "Padre, when will this crazy world settle down? This sort of thing will get us nowhere."

He was greatly disturbed and I tried to calm him. Then my Calvinism came to the fore, and I said, "Soldier, never forget that God still rules and over-rules the affairs of men."

He looked at me like a man who had been shot and said somewhat whimsically and wistfully, "Say, Padre, what have you got that I haven't got?" That question, not always in these same words, is asked sooner or later of every minister as he stands up to preach. Modern man has a right to know the rock upon which we stand and the faith by which we live.

The roots of life are nourished in the soil of a living faith; and when that soil becomes sour, the roots wither and the tree perishes. The seeds of decay are never in external forces, but in the lack of inner resources. Lord Morley in his incomparable biography of William Gladstone quotes a sentence which the British statesman wrote in his diary when he was a boy of twenty-one: "That the life of God may become the habit of my soul." During all the years of his life he held fast to it and never departed from it a hair's breadth. Years later when Lord Roseberry assumed the reins of government, he said: "To those who were privileged to enjoy his friendship, politics was the least important thing in him. But the most important part to which all other things were subservient was his religion."

It is something of that which must come back to our blundering world. How can we maintain our freedom and save ourselves from the perils of a planned economy; how can we increase international good will; how can we make our cities free from poverty and our streets free from crime if we push out of our thinking the ageless confession of the Christian Church, "I believe in God the Father Almighty, Maker of heaven and earth"?

I recall the last Army camp which I visited before the war. A notice had been posted that two regiments were to march out before dawn to the edge of the camp to listen to a lecture by a distinguished Army officer, returned from overseas duty, on the subject of how to take a military objective. Early the next morning I marched out with them, and we sat down in the long, wet grass on the side of a hill. At the foot of the hill stood this Army officer, who first described the wrong way of reaching an objective, and then he had it demonstrated. After that he told us the right way of taking an objective. He had it demonstrated in this fashion:

To our left, out of a clump of trees there came a platoon of soldiers. You could hardly see them in the early dawn. They fell on their hands and knees, hugging the soil and clinging close to the sod. So they crept through the long, lush, wet grass and were almost indistinguishable. Then somewhat causally the commanding officer called up to us, "When you advance on your knees, you are always safe."

That simple sentence should be written on the lintels of every home and carved on the threshold of every school and factory. Life would be strangely emancipated from frustration, insignificance, and fear if men everywhere could discover that assurance.

Almost one hundred years ago Renan, whom you cannot call Christian by the wildest stretch of the imagination, made this forecast, "I predict that the twentieth century will spend a great deal of its time picking out of the wastebasket things which the nineteenth century threw into it." What a startling prophecy that was, and how grim has been its fulfillment. What rummaging there has been in the wastebasket for those things which the near past tossed into it as having no meaning. And the one thing above all other things for which this blundering age is seeking amid the so-called outworn trumperies of yesterday is belief in a God of love.

When the preacher goes back to that message, he will once again become the molder of men and maker of a new tomorrow. It is so easy for the modern preacher to go off on tangents, trying to cure a malady without removing the cause. A man's creative influence is not measured by the number of things he accomplishes but rather by the quality of his response to life. To keep a tree green and growing something more is needed than trimming the branches and spraying the twigs. Carlyle was right: "A new splendor of God must come to the heart of this industrial age." If water trickling out of a spring is unwholesome, there is only one cure: the spring must be purified. If bitter water runs through a river, you cannot sweeten it by planting rose bushes on the river bank. If the center of life is sound, the whole life will be pervaded by health. The heart of reform is the reform of the heart. That has been the message of the Church, with which it has marched triumphantly through the centuries.

I have a little summer home in the northern part of New York, just this side of the Canadian border, on the shores of Lake Ontario. Perhaps I can more accurately describe it when I tell you that it is a large fireplace with a little house built around it. One summer I was invariably awakened at dawn by a flicker who proceeded without interruption to peck away at the copper gutter along the edge of the steep roof. It was becoming a dreadful nuisance. Yet every morning the flicker was at it. He was getting nowhere fast, but he kept right on going. It was motion without results. It attracted attention but actually served no useful purpose. So much of preaching is of that character.

74

It concerns itself with things which lie on the circumference. It forgets the thing which lies at the center. And because that which lies on the circumference has taken the place of that which lies in the center, it fails to have power and influence.

Not many would doubt that one of the obvious and ominous signs of the times is disintegration. We seem to live in a world which is falling apart. When you inquire about the reasons for all that, you are told it is due to social maladjustments, crackpot ideologies, and economical injustices. All that may be true, but it goes much deeper than that. There is wanting today a fundamental sense of what lies at the center of life. When the lights go out and life tumbles in like a house of cards, when it is touch and go, man wants something more than pleasing dissertations and homilies on the things which lie on the surface of life. How desperately the age needs the preaching of the assurance that a God of love stands in the center of the universe and that this God of love is seeking to reconcile the world through Jesus Christ our Lord!

Man can never find peace by repeating the sentence of the creed, "I believe in God the Father Almighty." He wants to know what bearing all this can have upon his day-by-day life. As one said to me not long ago, "In some down-to-earth language, what does it mean to repeat that sentence?" I want to suggest that those who hold that statement of faith live with three simple convictions.

First, it means that there rests upon life a sense of divine *kinship*. God is our Father. We are his children. Man is made in the divine image. We are fashioned after his likeness. That image of God in man can never be completely destroyed. No one can take it away from you. There is no grave of evil deep enough; there is no darkness black enough to take it away from you. No one can rob you of it. You may deface the image of God, but you cannot ultimately efface it. Do you know one of the oldest legends that has come down through the tumbling of the centuries? Strangely enough, it is a legend about creation.

One day four seeds presented themselves to God, who asked them what they wanted to become. The first seed said, "I like water, and there is so much of it in the world. If I could swim, then I could go everywhere on the earth. If I had fins, then I could swim."

God said, "Very well, I will make you a fish."

Then came the second seed and said, "I do not like water, but I like air. I do not like to swim, but I like to fly. I do not want fins, but I want wings."

Then God said, "I will make you a bird."

The third seed said, "I do not like water, and I do not like air, but I like the jungle. I do not like to swim; I do not like to fly; but I like to travel through the jungle. I do not want fins; I do not want wings; but I would like to have claws and teeth."

And God said, "I will make you a tiger."

Then the fourth seed came and said in great modesty, "I do not like water or air or the jungle. I do not want fins or wings or claws. But make me like yourself, and I will take my chances that way."

Then God smiled and said, "Very well, I will make you a man."

Believe me, most of us would rid life of the sense of defeatism if we could once again recover the assurance that we are forever and forever the children of God, and that we have a kinship with him whom we call Father. Just try living with that conviction for one day, and see what a difference it will make in your life.

Again, the conviction that a God of love stands in the center of the universe means that there rests upon life a sense of divine *purpose*. Huxley once said, "When I go to engage lodgings I do not say, 'Madam, where is the room located, how many windows has it, and what is the charge?' No, rather, I go to her asking, 'Madam, what is your view of the universe?'" Then he adds somewhat naïvely, "If she is right there, she will be right in everything; if she is wrong there, it doesn't matter what she says about other things." You see, it makes all the difference in the world what you believe to stand central in life and in the universe.

Life has a mission for everyone. We march to some predestined end. Nothing walks with aimless feet. Man is not like the horses in a chariot race on the stage of a theater, running furiously but getting nowhere fast. Through every incident and episode there runs a divine purpose. The very fact that you live implies a mission which no one else can fulfill but yourself. If you fail in your mission, it will go undone. It means that history is coming out somewhere, and that the universe is not a dead-end street. This is a world of law and order. It is not a kind of world in which the rules are one thing one day and something else another day. No one could live in a world like that. How far would you get if the sun rose sometimes in the east and sometimes in the northwest? How far would you go if sometimes, when you sowed violet seeds, your harvest were poison ivy? How far could you get in this world if the law of gravitation worked sometimes in the reverse? No, it is a sense of divine purpose and law which undergirds life.

When you really lay hold upon that simple fact, you can act as if you have nothing to lose and live as though nothing can throw you. We are in the keeping of God, who holds us with a love that will not let us go, whose purpose shall be accomplished. His plans may be deferred, but they cannot be defeated; they may be postponed, but they cannot be crushed.

Albert Payson Terhune, the inimitable writer of dog stories, toward the end of his life made a contract with a New York publisher to write a book on immortality. No one knew that he was writing this book, not even members of his family. After his death the publisher made representation to the family for the manuscript. They were not aware of its existence at all, but rummaging among his effects they found this incomplete manuscript, like an unfinishd symphony, on life after death. I shall never forget the day that I was permitted to read it. It is rather significant that the last sentence of the last paragraph of his treatise on immortality was this: "God always finishes his sentences."

If somehow that simple fact could be realized today, most people could be cured of their frustration, fear and despair. So many today are suffering from defeatism. They make their own the cruel observation of Marcus Aurelius,

"This, too, will pass away." Here and there you meet a radiant life, blessed be God, but all too often people like that are as an island in a sea of despair. Now and again you will hear someone say with Coleridge, "O God, how wonderful it is to live." But more often men are apt to chant the miserere of Renan, "O God, if there be a God, when will life be worth living?" The age today is desperately disillusioned. Hope has slipped through men's fingers as water filters through the finger tips of a statue in a garden fountain. Men are disposed to believe that disease will always ravage, that pain will always prevail, that ignorance will always have a toe hold, and that the four horsemen of the Apocalypse will always ride. If life could recover today not simply the sense of divine kinship, but of divine purpose, the chords that are broken would vibrate once more.

Once again, the assurance that a God of love stands in the center of the universe means that there rests upon life a sense of divine *presence*. God is not simply an isolated being, the first cause of all that exists. God is not simply dualism, a spiritual force fighting a hopeless battle with formless chaos. God is not simple pantheism, in which the whole world is a cruel unfolding of an impersonal creator. God is not simply a creator tumbling stars into space, organizing seasons and tides and skylarks and mountains. When life tumbles out of nowhere into somewhere and begins its long pilgrimage, God does not bow himself out of it. When life begins its long journey down the river of time to the ocean of eternity, God does not abandon it or beach it.

As surely as the spirit of God brooded upon the formless

chaos in the hour of creation and as surely as the pilgrims to Emmaus had the companionship of Christ, so surely does God's presence go with you every day for ever and ever. He cares what happens to the reed that is broken and bent, to the lily that fades, to the sheep that is lost, and to the prodigal who steps across the threshold of indiscretion. Zangwill in his *Cockpit* makes one of his characters say, "It must be a terrible thing to be God. Sometimes when I cannot sleep, I think of the eternal insomnia of the Almighty." Well, we have a God like that. Over the breaking waves of the sea of time comes the golden glow, "Lo, I am with you alway even unto the end."

The good Shepherd never abandons his sheep when they are caught in brambles. He is never petulant or impatient when they run away. With a sharp eye he looks over his flock for cuts and bruises. When he sees an injury, he heals the torn flesh with oil out of his horn. When they are trapped in a crevice, he lifts them out with his shepherd's crook. When they are exhausted, he dips into his water bag and slakes their thirst. At the end of the day when night comes, he brings them back to some secure enclosure, where he stands guard over them, keeping silent vigil until the morning comes.

That is the picture of this eternal God, the unwearying Shepherd. He is not an absentee landlord. He does not sit, like some eternal Buddha, with his eyes shut and arms folded. I asked an architect recently if he ever went back to the buildings which he had designed and erected. He replied, "When once my work is finished and I have been paid, I almost never go back to see it. After the contract is finished, I lose interest in it." God is not like that.

Admiral Richard E. Byrd in his book *Alone* recalls what he lived through in that lonely advance outpost where he stayed alone for many long weary months and was almost overcome by gas poisoning. Let me quote these lines:

About 3 o'clock on the morning of June 2nd, I had another lucid phase. I tried without success to force my body into sleep. The sleeping pills were on the shelf. The flashlight fingered the bottle. . . . I reached for the bottle. But then I stopped. It was impossible to go on like this. . . . I found a match and lighted a candle. An unused sheet of paper lay on the bunk, on top of the diary. I wrote: "The universe is not dead. Therefore, there is an Intelligence there, and it is all pervading. . . . The human race, then, is not alone in the universe. Though I am cut off from human beings, *I* am not alone." Dousing the candle, I slipped into the bag, and repeated the sentiments over and over again. Sleep came after a while.[1]

It is this miracle of grace which comes to those who live with a consciousness of the keeping of God. Believe me, this conviction that a God of love stands in the center of the universe has everything to do with successful living.

Let me make one more observation about the significance of this central message that a God of love stands in the center of the universe. Someone will say, "All that is very well, but what becomes of the social gospel on that basis?" What possible bearing can it have upon the economic, so-

[1] Copyright 1938 by Richard E. Byrd. Used by permission of the publishers, G. P. Putnam's Sons.

cial, political, and international problems of mankind? Well, let us see.

It becomes the most creative force in life. It has tremendous implications. Indeed, it is the most revolutionary and explosive force that has ever come into the world. When a person believes that a God of love stands in the center of the universe, he will care what happens to God's world, and what is more significant, he will care what happens to God's children.

I stood one day at a little cottage in Lanarkshire, Scotland. Many years ago the family living in that house then had arisen early to bid farewell to a son. After a frugal breakfast they read the 121st psalm and offered a prayer. Then the son walked out of his home, tramped to Glasgow, and took a ship to Central Africa. Years later they found him dead upon his knees by a handmade cot in a tiny hut in the long-grass jungle country of Africa. Natives carried his body two thousand miles over rivers and mountains and through jungles until it was placed in a tomb in Westminster Abbey to become England's greatest missionary hero of the nineteenth century. How can you argue from a beginning so humble to a grave so illustrious? David Livingstone had written across his life, "I put no values upon anything I possess save in terms of the kingdom of God." It was the creative force of the gospel of God which changed him, and through which he brought light and hope to a dark continent.

It is still so today. Take it in this matter of hunger. Two thirds of the world is going to bed hungry tonight. When you think of that, food almost chokes in your throat at mealtimes, and you can't swallow. Believe me, if war comes, which God forbid, it will not be due to political chicanery or diplomatic double talk, but it will be due to hunger. Hunger does queer things to people. Whether or not we have peace or war in the world of the near future largely depends, therefore, upon food. We have it in our power, by reason of our great supply of food and grain, to determine our own destiny and that of the world. The man who sees that a God of love stands in the center of the universe will want to do something about this hunger.

I do not pretend to know all the answers, but I do know one. When that war ended we said, "We have liberated the continent, now let them shift for themselves." We came back on our transports and pulled the door shut after us. Tragically it hasn't worked out very well, for another generation has had to do it all over again. What this world needs desperately today is the recovery of a conviction that a God of love stands at the center of the universe, whose children we all, all are. He plays no favorites. He does not separate people by the barbed-wire entanglements of political or geographic frontiers. The way to a world of peace, believe me, will never be solved by sinking atomic bombs in the depth of the sea or exploding them in the air but by recognizing again that we are children of our heavenly Father.

Take it in the matter of housing and slum clearance. I once lived in a city in which oftentimes five thousand people lived in a block. Their intolerable quarters are rented on the stagger system. One family will occupy it for a half a day and then go out in the streets to shift for themselves while another family moves in for its share of twelve hours. How can we tolerate slums and ghettos before the simple fact we are God's children? Don't you think that God cares about things like that?

I have among my friends a very distinguished engineer who has blueprinted and brought to a consummation some fine housing projects. I asked him some time ago what effect this new housing had upon the day-by-day life of people. He told me a very interesting fact. When the blueprints had been prepared for one of these developments, he petitioned the board of education to build a new school as part of that project. He offered the board of education the gift of land in that development upon which they could erect a school. After some investigation the board declined the offer. They thought it was simply a clever scheme on the part of the builders to entice people into this area on the basis that they would have a new school. The board had made a survey of the number of children in families of the low-income group which were to be housed in this development. They discovered that the average family unit included one-half of a child. On that basis there were schools enough in that area.

What actually happened was this: A year and a half after the completion of this development in which families lived in comfort, with light and playing fields and fresh air and sunshine, the number of children per family unit had increased to one and one-half children. If we could see again this God of love, we would have interest in these housing developments. Don't you think that God cares what happens? Do you not see how this fundamental conviction has everything to do with the everyday life of people?

Do you know the poetry of Father Tabb? He is one of those lovable men in the field of religion who expresses his mystical faith not in terms of form or ritual but in terms of words. One day he was walking through the streets of Baltimore when he saw a little boy bouncing a rubber ball back and forth between the open palm of his hand and the sidewalk. Suddenly a gust of wind blew the ball out of control and rolled it into the traffic of the street, where it was destroyed. Great heart that he was, Father Tabb walked up to the sobbing boy, put his arms around him, and quieted him. Then he walked back to his study and wrote these lines:

> A little Boy of heavenly birth,
>   But far from home to-day,
> Comes down to find His ball, the Earth,
>   That Sin had cast away.
> O comrades let us one and all
> Join in to get Him back His ball!

V. The Lost Sense of Wonder

LONG CENTURIES AGO AN UNKNOWN POET WROTE AN ALMOST forgotten poem on the subject of the forgotten man. In language which melts one to tears, and in words which strangely warm the heart, he sang of the goodness of God to the forgotten of men. That poem sounds like the music of far-off waterfalls to all who find themselves abandoned by men, forgotten by their generation, or beached upon the lonely shores of time by some cruel and relentless fate. Listen to some of the sentences: "He healeth the broken in heart and bindeth up their wounds. He telleth the number of the stars; he calleth them all by their names. . . . He giveth to the beast his food, and to the young ravens which cry. . . . He gathereth together the outcasts."

Now in the very center of this hymn to the goodness of God to the forgotten of men you come upon this: "Who maketh grass to grow upon the mountains." What an astonishing and fantastic sentence! That is the very place where grass does not grow. Meadows always thin out as you approach the top of a mountain. Green fields are associated with lowlands and valleys and watercourses and oases. Lush grass always disappears beyond the timber belt. But there it was, and the poet saw it.

86

So as he sang his hymn to the goodness of God to the forgotten of men, he added this line to the God of the incredible. Things which seemingly have no chance do get their chance. What no one believed possible he brings to pass. What seemingly could not occur does take place. The things which could not happen he brings into being. He walks along unanticipated paths, and he traces courses you cannot plot. You can never tell at what bend of the road he will meet you. That is why the religious life is so full of romance. You meet him where you least expect him. So the poet urges people to live with an eager, alert, and expectant faith. Life is always encompassed by the sense of wonder and mystery.

There are unfortunate people who think only of what has been. They worship at the shrine of the *status quo*. They believe what has been, is; and what is, will be, "World without end." Such people are always cynical and frustrated, about as comfortable to live with as a sand tick. But there are other people, and we bless God for them, who never lose sight of tomorrow. They are determined not to let things happen, but to make them happen. They face the dawn and live with an eager and expectant faith. Such people are the hope of the world today. If ever the kingdom of God is to come, ushering in a braver and better order, it will be because of those who were determined to bring it to pass, however difficult and hopeless that adventure may seem at this hour.

Those who live with a faith in the God of the incredible are always vindicated by history. Two thousand years ago a handful of men started out upon a fantastic mission.

They addressed themselves to the solemn task of building a world without pain, without panic, without disease; a world in which childhood would not be forgotten, womanhood not neglected, and old age not abandoned; a world in which man would come before the machine, and personality before profits; a world in which man's inhumanity to man would be supplanted by the law that we are our brothers' keepers; a world in which the four horsemen of the Apocalypse would never again ride. All that and infinitely more is what they meant when they prayed, "Thy kingdom come." They had no publicity agents to advertise them, no wealthy friends to intercede for them, no political leaders to plead their cause. They had nothing but an undaunted faith in a God who does the incredible. And yet such is the vindication of history that within sixty generations this little handful of men has come to include one third of the population of the modern world, building a Church upon which the sun never sets. God, who makes grass to grow upon the mountains and is forever doing the impossible, made their dream come true.

There was that time when a whole new political structure was established upon these shores. It was a new way of living together, called democracy. We speak of it today as the American way of life. That too seemed a fantastic dream. When it had been launched, Matthew Arnold came from England to study and to evaluate this movement. After he had traveled up and down and surveyed the movement at close range, he went back and laughed, saying that it would not outlive the generations which had brought it into being. But the God who does the incredible and makes grass to grow upon the mountains was with this little handful of simple people upon New England's broken coast. Today that little group has become one of the mightiest nations of all times, of which the whole world stands in either fear or hope. History always vindicates the faith of those who believe in the God of the incredible.

One day Rousseau wrote a book which stirred the imagination of the common people. It had to do with the social contrasts of the time. He laid down the simple fact that nations are judged by what happens to the man at the bottom of the ladder. He made a plea for the underprivileged and tried to quicken the conscience of his generation for the poor and needy. The world read the book and laughed, because they were sure nothing could come of it. But years later, when Carlyle looked back upon the critics of the book, he wrote, "Their skins went into the making of the second edition." History always vindicates those who live with a faith in the impossible.

The stones which the builders reject have a strange way of becoming the headstones of the corners. Dead issues and lost causes have a strange way of becoming alive. What could not happen, does happen, and what seemed impossible prevails. This is the supreme lesson of history. Those who put their trust in God are never put to shame.

This is true not only in history but also in the realm of biography. Domremy was a second-class village in France. The people who lived there were for the most part dull and stupid. They seemed to have no future. Nobody expected anything to come out of a setting like that. But the God who makes the grass to grow upon the mountains was walking through the dull setting of that village, and Joan of Arc walked into immortality as the saviour of France.

On Pigeon Creek in Indiana, on the edge of a clearing, there once stood a small cabin. It was in reality a three-wall enclosure, fourteen feet square, where a tall gaunt boy with coon-skin cap read borrowed books before the fireplace. Near by was a school which the boy in the coon-skin cap attended for six or nine months. The schoolmaster petitioned the authorities and urged his friends to secure for him a transfer because he was dealing with such unlikely material. He saw no chance for those who came there. And yet all the while there sat in front of him a boy who became the kind of man God gives to the world once in five hundred years—Abraham Lincoln. Biography is forever vindicating the faith of those who believe in the impossible.

I have said all this because we desperately need today a recovery of that conviction. We belong to a generation which is suffering from one thing above all other things: it is the lost sense of wonder. We no longer believe that the impossible can happen, and that the things which have no chance can come to pass. You see that in the world of affairs. We have just fought and won the war for freedom. By the grace of God the forces of freedom prevailed while the forces of totalitarianism were totally and deservingly defeated. One would suppose that a sigh of relief would run through this world, and that the fires of hope and joy would be burning bright. Now as a matter of fact, what must be obvious to all, the very opposite is the truth. We are living in a world which is slinking back into sullen moods, sour tempers, bickering cynicisms. Indeed, more than any other generation we seem to be haunted by frustration. A strange kind of irrationality seems to rest upon everything. We are uncertain; we do not know who or what to believe.

Take it in the matter of this search for one world. After long and painstaking searching the statesmen of the world brought into being the United Nations Organization. It is the expression of the hope and the conscience of the people of this world. It is an instrument for living together in good will and understanding. Yet, strangely enough, we are already beginning to despair of the superstructure long before we have finished laying the foundations. We have not even given decent burial to the dead of the last war, and we are already talking about a Third World War. We seem to be overwhelmed with cynicism bordering on despair.

What ails us? Why has all this happened to us? We have lost sight of the God who makes grass to grow upon the mountains and brings into being what seemingly has no chance. A better tomorrow can come if we are willing to pay the price. You have only to read Lecky's *History of European Morals* and Latourette's *Anno Domini* to realize that what nobody believed would come to pass, does come to pass. If we knew history better, we would not be so overwhelmed by the defeatist mind. If somehow we could have a fresh baptism or rebirth of faith in the God of the incredible, we would meet the future with greater serenity and courage. There is hope for an age which holds the door open, but there is no hope for an age which pulls the door shut. There is hope for those who say, "It may be," but there is no hope for those who say, "Never."

Then, too, we need desperately the recovery of this kind of faith in the realm of religion. The sense of defeatism has been upon the Church for a long time. Organized religion has had its back to the wall; the tides have been running out on it. In the so-called conflict between science and religion, religion has always been compelled to give ground. Religion deals with the eternal while science deals with the temporary; but the eternal has always been compelled to yield to the temporary. Religion deals with truth while science deals with information; but truth has always been compelled to bow and scrape before information. The great affirmations of religion have been petulantly swept aside. It has been popular to disavow the transcendence of God, the meaning of Calvary, and the fact of the Resurrection. We are told you can no longer believe that he fed the hungry and healed the sick and raised the dead. Faith is supposed to be the fiction of the feeling of inferiority. The modern intellectual thinks of prayer as a kind of spiritual autointoxication. Religion is held to be an escape mechanism, a running away from reality. It has ruthlessly discredited the supernatural and the invisible. The result is that the finite has supplanted the infinite and the creature has taken the place of the creator.

Once upon a time man said, "Speak, Lord; for thy servant heareth." Today he is apt to say, "Listen, God, man is talking." One does not often come upon a vibrant and vital faith in the God who brings the impossible to pass. The result is that many are making all manner of compromises, reducing the Christian faith to a kind of sublimating humanism. For that reason many no longer take organized religion seriously, and the influence of the Church wanes.

But we need the recovery of this lost sense of wonder not only in the realm of world affairs and in the area of religion, but also in the field of human personality. There are times when we are overwhelmed by life. Ask any physician or minister who counsels with people what is the usual attitude toward life, and he will tell you that people are becoming problems to themselves. Many have made themselves believe that they do not count. They are sure the world has passed them by. Great movements are surging through the world, but they believe they will never have a part in them. It is a tragic sense of defeatism and insignificance which grips so many today. For all their struggling, they seem "no painful inch to gain." Relentless forces are driving them to the very edge of despair. They are entangled by their own ennui. They know what will work and what will not work, yet they proceed to follow through the things that will not work. Nothing matters. The sense of the importance of life has gone out of them.

What can you do for people like that? And what has religion to say to them? Place that attitude side by side with the God of the incredible, who can make the impossible come to pass; and suddenly redemptive forces begin to work in the human soul, emancipating him from fear, releasing him from frustration, and breaking the galling chains of insignificance. It turns weakness into strength, miserliness into magnanimity, and callousness into compassion. It will make the drunkard sober; it will make the miser magnanimous; it will make the sinner a saint. That is the glory of the Christian gospel. That is what we mean by conversion. Would God it might happen to someone who reads these lines. There is no issue so forlorn he cannot bring to triumph; there is no cause so hopeless he cannot lead to victory; there is no toil so commonplace he cannot glorify; there is no life so soiled or stained he cannot make clean.

> Isn't it strange
> That princes and kings,
> And clowns that caper
> In sawdust rings,
> And common people
> Like you and me
> Are builders for eternity?

When you hold fast to the assurance that God makes grass to grow upon the mountains, nothing can throw you. You can act as if you have nothing to lose; you can live as though nothing can defeat you. It was this simple faith which sustained the early Christians through the agonizing and insufferable years of persecution. When this faith has been recovered, the Church will once again have the power and vitality it had in olden days.

There are these unforgettable lines of Miriam Teichner:

> God—let me be aware.
> Let me not stumble blindly down the ways,
> Just getting somehow safely through the days,
> Not even groping for another hand,
> Not even wondering why it all was planned,
> Eyes to the ground unseeking for the light,
> Soul never aching for a wild-winged flight,
> Please, keep me eager just to do my share.
> God—let me be aware.

VI. The Protestant Witness

WE ARE WITNESSING TODAY A NEW CHALLENGE TO PROTES-
tantism, into the inheritance of which, by the grace of God,
many of us have entered. It is having a hard time of it. Protestantism by and large has its back to the wall, and the
tides are running out on it. It is rather significant that when
democracy finds it difficult to survive, Protestantism suffers
with it. They are inter-related; what affects one, affects the
other. Both have come to the difficult and disturbing challenge of authoritarianism. If we are to meet this insistent
determined challenge with any degree of intelligence and
convictions, we shall have to give an account of the faith
that is in us and know upon what it rests.

What are the causes behind this challenge; does Protestantism bear witness to something distinct and unique;
has it a relevance for our time or is it a spent force? If
we can give a reasonable answer to these questions, many
of the misgivings will be resolved and the fires of faith
rekindled in the Protestant fellowship.

Let us begin by stating quite frankly there are those
who feel that Protestantism has no meaning and no dis-
tinctive message for our time. They seem to think it stands
for nothing in particular. They have lost their enthusiasm

for it. The faith of their fathers no longer thrills them, nor does the Church's statements of faith make their pulses beat faster. Indeed, these lukewarm and timid souls have lost their pride in it. They apologize for it, but they do not defend it. They look upon the whole thing with great regret without being able to tell exactly why. They regard Protestantism as a perfect illustration of historic blundering: the inevitable product of an intolerant age. If the same crisis were to face us today, no such schism would ever come to pass. So these well-meaning but misguided critics indulge in the luxury of vagueness.

Then, too, there are others who have concluded that while Protestantism once made a contribution, it no longer has a functioning purpose. There was a time when man was fighting for his freedom and individuality. Then Protestantism stood him in good stead and was profoundly relevant. It helped him break the shackles. It had a message in the day when an emphasis upon individualism was needed. But this is a different world. The age is marked by mass movements, co-operation, and social solidarity. Not individualism, but socialism is in the forefront of man's thinking. Protestantism inherently does not fit into that mood and mold. Doubtless it had a place in an age when individualism was to the fore. But isolated individualism is unable to cope with the complicated and complex structure of society. They maintain, therefore, that Protestantism has run its course and served its purpose, and we must bid it farewell. The future of the world is in some other expression of Christian faith.

There are still others who are quite convinced that Protestantism has no contribution to make today because of its hopeless divisions. It is a religious fellowship torn by deep strife. Instead of fighting evil, it has come to fight itself. It hates a shade of truth more than it hates error. If one little sect makes a proposal, it will be opposed by the second sect because the idea did not originate with them. They have concluded that Protestantism has fallen apart into a series of bickering groups, each seeking some advantage at the expense of the other. It has no leadership to offer in the day when the demand for "one world" is abroad. A divided world can never be healed by divided Protestantism. So for one reason or another many have lost faith in the enterprise. Those who still hold fast to it are often like the child who whistles in the dark to keep up his courage.

I, for one, hold no such fears. The attitude of defeatism is utterly unwarranted and unworthy. We can stand with this faith of our fathers before this or any age unashamed and unafraid. If there could be restored to the Protestant Church that sense of devotion and courage which brought it into being, Protestantism would once again burn like a torch and shine like a star.

There is one more fact which we should have before us. Raising one's voice in defense of Protestantism does not necessarily involve decrying other expressions of the Christian faith. There are unfortunate people who think they cannot speak a good word for their own country unless in the same breath they speak caustically of every other country. I have never thought that attitude worthy

97

of a true citizen. The person who thinks that he can only defend his own political ideals by damaging the political convictions of other men shows an inherent weakness. That is equally true in religion. I hope I shall never raise my voice in anything that deepens and intensifies estrangements in Christendom. There are many highways that lead to Christ. What we are doing here is bearing testimony to the highway we are traveling and making clear the reasons why we find it the satisfying way. The true Christian should be a builder of bridges, not barricades. We will never advance Protestantism by discrediting the faith of those who differ with us. There is enough faultfinding, intolerance, and bigotry in the world without the Protestant Church joining the anvil chorus. You never solve problems by calling people names.

Protestantism gratefully acknowledges its debt of gratitude to the Jew. There is no understanding of the New Testament apart from the Old Testament. Indeed, ours is the only major religion whose Bible contains the sacred literature of two religions. Ours is a Judean-Christian faith. We acknowledge our debt to the Jew, who has given us our sense of God who is holy and just. He has given us the conviction that we live in a universe in which right is always right and wrong is always wrong. He has kept alive in the world the assurance that history is coming out somewhere, and that the universe is not a dead-end street. He has emphasized the importance of a moral content and spiritual basis for life. He has enriched us with his matchless psalms and hopes. Through the Psalms he built for us roads of prayer and adoration over which we have traveled to the God of all grace.

Then, too, we gratefully acknowledge our debt of gratitude to the Catholic. For two thousand years we have repeated together the Lord's Prayer. For fifteen hundred years we have recited in unison the common confession of our Christian faith called the Apostles' Creed. Together we believe in the Atonement, the Incarnation, the Resurrection, and the triumph of the kingdom of God. We share with him two sacraments. We read the same New Testament, and often we sing the same hymns. He keeps reminding us of the beauty of worship. He has kept the Cross central. We are rooted and grounded in the same fundamental truth. Out of the Catholic Church there have come pious and saintly people who have been as lights to their several generations. We bless God for them. Protestantism in its debt to the Jew and the Catholic has always held fast to the saying of Paul, "Ye . . . are built upon the foundation of the apostles and prophets."

But while we have many things in common with the faith of the Jew and Catholic, it is also true that we have certain distinct differences. While there are many elements of similarity, there are also elements of dissimilarity which constitute our heritage. Protestantism is something more than a negation. It is not simply a fellowship of people who decry what is missing in the faith of another group. One can never build a church on a negation. While it came into being as a protest against certain obvious shortcomings in organized Christianity of that time, it immediately announced certain affirmations by which its followers proposed to live. It was essentially a determination to return to the warm evangelical faith of the first century. It is a recovery of a forgotten emphasis. One might well call it a revival of the gospel pattern. It brought back something Christendom cannot afford to lose. Protestantism has been as leaven in the meal. Even the Roman Church has been cleansed of much of its dross because of the birth of this Protestant fellowship. Indeed, where Protestantism is strong, the Roman Church is always at its best and purest. Where Protestantism does not exist or is very weak, there the Roman Church always reveals its worst and most regrettable features.

Why is that so? What are the convictions upon which the Protestant fellowship is based? What are the fundamental affirmations to which it bears witness and by which it must be judged?

Protestantism affirms that the Bible is the only rule and guide of faith and practice. The Bible is to us the final court of appeal. If we are asked why do we believe thus and so, the answer is, "Because it is in the Book." That Book stands central. There may not be everywhere in Protestantism a full agreement upon its content or structure. There may be differing opinions as to who wrote what and why. After all, you cannot force fixed patterns upon the entire Christian fellowship. But whether the Bible "is" or "contains" the Word of God, the fact to which we bear witness is that God has spoken to us through that Book. It is not a comprehensive system of philosophy or doctrine. It is rather a book in which men record their experiences with

God. Within the pages of this Book man speaks to God and God speaks to man. It is the record of what God has done for man at certain times in history and at certain places in the world. It is the revealing of the acts of God and the unveiling of his purpose in history. It is the highway over which man has traveled to God and down which God has come to man. It comes to focus in Jesus Christ, who is the Word made flesh.

For us, therefore, the Book is a lamp to our feet and a light upon our path. It is the rainbow on the cloud and an anchor in a storm. It is the pillar of hope in the night of despair, and the cloud of comfort in the blazing of tension and pain. We are a people who believe in saturating our language with its vocabulary, our minds with its truth, our hearts with its love. Where men have come to know it and understand it, life has been enriched and deepened. When the Bible is neglected, sooner or later something goes out of life. We are a people of the Book and with the Book.

Protestantism affirms that we are children of God and therefore have access to him at all times. Man is made in his likeness and fashioned after his image. No one can take it from you. With joy and confidence we may say, "My Father." Paul suggested that long ago: In Christ Jesus we have access to God with confidence. We have peace with God through Jesus Christ our Lord.

God is our Father and we are his children. We are free to enter into his presence. In a foreign country a citizen cannot go to the ruler of another country except through his appointed ambassador. There is no direct access of the citizen of one country to the ruler of another except through that embassy. But ours is not such a relation. We may come to God in terms of home. Just as every child can go without fear to its father, so may we come to God. We do not need an intermediary. It is not necessary to go to some ecclesiastical authority or official. We do not have to seek some person to bring us to him. You can go to him and say, "Here, God, poor and needy, I stand." All are priests before him, and every person is a guardian of his own conscience.

How that simple fact breaks the bonds of fear and frustration! Because we are children of God, we can live joyfully in his world. No one can take that relation from us. It makes of life a thrilling adventure and gives us joy and peace and strength. Those who are most aware of this relationship with God are completely emancipated from the things that keep many people in bondage. By the same token, because we yield ourselves to God and belong to him, no other person on earth has the right to claim us. We do not need to bend our knee to any other master.

Those who belong to this fellowship have always been the bulwark of freedom. Spiritual emancipation has led to political freedom. Those who confess, "We know no king but thee, O God" have always refused to bow the knee to tyrants. We surrender our wills to him but to no other. No authority on earth can compel our allegiance. That is why Protestantism has always synchronized with democracy. We are the sons of God, and Christ has made us free. There is no authority on earth great enough to stifle our conscience. Those who make light of Protestantism may well ponder the fact that the birth of this Protestant fellowship brought into existence the free press, the free ballot, free speech, and freedom of religious worship. Wherever men have held fast to this conviction tyranny has been overthrown. It is a rather significant fact that the leaders of the underground and resistance movements of much of the Continent during the last cruel war came largely out of the Protestant fellowship. Wherever man is conscious of his sonship with God, there comes also a new dignity to life, which he will not permit external forces to soil. The highest expressions of democracy have come in those countries where Protestantism is strongest. This great conviction was expressed later in terms of political life, "we hold these truths to be self-evident, that all men are created equal." The Protestant fellowship has not only demanded and paid the price for freedom but has also been the champion of the oppressed. Everywhere it has come to the defense of minorities. It has lifted its voice in no uncertain terms against racial prejudices, and class consciousness. Where Protestantism prevails, religious minorities always have their rights.

Protestantism affirms that our redemption comes not by way of good deeds, but by way of a self-surrendered life. The poignant search of all ages has been for some method of getting rid of sin. The eternal question which has cut through the unbroken centuries is, "What must I do to be saved?" Man is haunted by the sense of estrangement from God and his better self. He is aware that something has raised barriers which separate him from God. Some years ago a missionary was preaching to a group of outcasts in a village in South India. He used lantern slides to depict

103

scenes and episodes in the life of Christ, which he would then explain. When he threw upon the white-washed mud wall the scene of the Crucifixion and explained its meaning, one of the outcasts walked up to the picture and called out, "Come down, Son of God; that is my place." That deep sense of guilt rests upon every human life, haunting him like a vice and following him like a shadow. The one thing above all other things he wants to know is how he can get rid of sin.

In the world in which Paul lived there was a cruel law for punishing transgressors. If a man was convicted of a crime and found guilty, the body of the murdered person was fastened to the back of the criminal with thongs and ropes. He could never take it off. He was never permitted to get rid of it. He was compelled to eat with it and sleep with it and live with it. He carried it about everywhere he went. Days and nights without end it remained strapped to his back, until the process of decomposition set in. It was a frightful punishment. One day Paul viewed this loathsome spectacle and said it was like that with sin, which made him cry out, "Oh wretched man that I am! who shall deliver me from the body of this death?" Yes, we all carry about with us this appalling sense of guilt. How can we get rid of it?

To all such, Protestantism calls out that our redemption comes not by way of good deeds but by way of self-surrendered life. It has caught up the watchcry which rings through the New Testament: "By grace are ye saved through faith; and that not of yourselves: it is the gift of God." The Protestant Church does not offer this redemption but proclaims it. It does not grant pardon; it bears witness to the assurance of pardon. It is not for the Church to give or to withhold this gift of God. Salvation is not vested in a self-perpetuating movement which assumes the right to give or to withhold it according to its own judgment. Redemption is not something which an institution can guarantee, nor is it something which we merit. Redemption is not something we earn but receive; it is not an achievement of man but a free gift of God. The barrier of sin which man has raised God has broken down through Christ. That is the meaning of salvation. God in his infinite love has offered to man a way out of his misery and frustration. This is the very heart of our evangel. It burns like a torch and shines like a star. It has proclaimed to all men everywhere the grace and goodness of God which we may expect through a self-surrendered will.

Protestantism affirms the oneness of all Christian believers. It is committed to keep the unity of spirit in the bond of peace. The Church is not a man-made structure; it is a fellowship of the twice-born. It is a comradeship of people who live with a sense of our oneness in Christ. It is held together by ties both human and divine. They share together the assurances and hopes of this common faith. Sometimes I fear too much has been made of this divisiveness in Protestantism. It is well to remember that most of the members of the Protestant Church are held together by very intimate ties of a common faith and hope. Indeed, 80 per cent of the Protestants in this country belong to six of the major portions of the Protestant Church.

And yet, let us affirm that its emphasis is not upon uniformity but unity. There is a vast difference between uniformity and unity. When the Catholic speaks of the oneness of the Church, he means uniformity. That is something external; it lies on the surface; it is a matter of outward patterns; it concerns itself with technique and regulations and institutions. But when the Protestant speaks of the oneness of the Church he is thinking of unity. That is something beneath the surface; it is a matter of heart and spirit; it rests not upon institutions but upon character. The oneness which we seek comes not through institutions but through a child-like trust and self-surrender.

This kind of unity, therefore, allows for diversity, and is much more genuine and vital than that which is enforced by external authority. Protestantism affirms a belief in the oneness of all Christian believers amid diversity. You have that in the world of nature. Nature, of course, is one. But nature is not the same. There is a vast difference between snowflakes and star clusters and rainbows and apple blossoms and tumbling tides. They are not alike, and yet nature is one. It is unity with diversity. You meet that also in human nature. Human nature is one, but people are different. Some are black; some are white; some are tall; some are short; some are red; some are yellow. People are different, but human nature is one. You have unity with diversity.

So it is in the Christian Church. We are one in Christ. But this too permits differing patterns. It is a good thing for an Episcopalian Church to have a Methodist Church near by to keep its heart warm. It does a Congregationalist good to come in touch with a Calvinist who has developed an organized system of belief. I would rather live in a New

England village with its three churches on the green, each giving friendly welcome to one and all, than to live in some village in Italy or Spain with its one church which may be utterly unconcerned or crassly indifferent to what happens to people. To us the Church is a fellowship of people who live a certain way of life. It is a comradeship with God and with man. It is a fellowship of people who are conscious of sin, seek forgiveness, and have found the grace of God in Christ. It is not an institution which is in the keeping of select and self-appointed groups; it is a fellowship of people, lay as well as clergy, in which all have a place and a meaning.

This, then, is the reason of the faith that is in us. Into this heritage, by the grace of God, we have entered, and we shall bear witness to it unashamed and unafraid. There may be other roads which lead to him, but for us this is a satisfying road. It is a costly road to travel. Believe me, great testings lie in the tomorrow of our lives. This is one of those either-or times, in which man cannot stand with his tongue in his cheek. Those who brought it into being were willing to pay the price. "These are they which came out of great tribulation, and have washed their robes and made them white in the blood of the lamb." This faith of our fathers to which we are committed is living still. We will be true to it to the end of the end. God make us worthy of the heritage which is ours. We may well commit ourselves to it anew in the words Bunyan wrote in his *Pilgrim's Progress* and with "stout countenances" say, "Set down my name, sir."

VII Words Are Not Enough

AUDIENCES OF ANY KIND ARE ALWAYS AFFECTED BY TWO things. The first is the setting of the preacher, and the second is the personality of the preacher. Each is important and both have their place. In the secular world theatrical people have long since become aware of the importance of the former. Ever so much attention is given to the stage setting, costumes, lighting, and scenery. Sometimes good plays fail because of the lack of proper setting, and sometimes an appealing stage setting will make successful a rather poor play. I recall one afternoon sitting with E. H. Sothern in his apartment. I noticed that he was pushing up the toes of an odd sort of sandal, trying to give it a curl upward. When I asked him what he was doing, he said, "These sandals are supposed to have a lift in the toe and look worn. The audience will think there is something wrong with my setting if they do not see it there."

What always impresses me in reading the story of the building of the temple in Old Testament life is the meticulous care with which every detail was planned. There is, for instance, a minute description of the vestments of the priests, the trumpets which were blown, the high altar, the huge cedar doors swinging on hinges of silver in sockets of gold, the cornices studded with Assyrian rosettes and the tops of the pillars carved with lily work. More than in the secular world are people affected by the setting. The Church of tomorrow must give much greater thought to all this. All too often church buildings have been so barren that they have failed to create an atmosphere of worship. I do not mean the glamorizing of the church, nor do I mean showmanship. But no one can question that much more thought and time should be given to the setting, if the preacher is to make effective his gospel. Because a church is drab is no reason to suppose it will create piety. Ugliness and bad ventilation are not necessary to saintliness.

But if audiences are affected by the setting of the preacher, they are much more affected by the personality of the preacher. "Personality" in itself is an interesting word. It comes from the two Latin words—*per* and *sonare*—meaning speaking through. The *persona* was a mask worn by actors on the Roman stage, to indicate the role they were playing. In many respects the preacher is the key to his own success. Whether or not what he says will leave an impact upon people often depends upon his own personality. If he is flippant and restless and inattentive, he will soon make his congregation cynical and indifferent and restless. The moment the minister enters the chancel every movement is observed. If his bearing is one of reverance, humility, and serenity, he will soon inspire reverence, humility, and sincerity.

One day Dr. Glover was addressing a group of divinity students before they went out on a preaching mission over a week end. He discussed with them how they should carry themselves. At the end he said, "Always remember the Incarnation." That simple statement leads to the very heart of this whole matter. You preach your sermons not simply from manuscript but from your life. Preaching by words is never enough.

Let me say something about that. I have already referred to the wistfulness of our times. People seem to have lost their perspective. They no longer know who or what to believe. A strange kind of irrationality is consuming our age. In a way there is nothing new about that wistfulness. Long centuries ago before the birth of Christ men cried, "Oh, that I knew where I might find him!" In that hour they turned to the prophets for guidance and hope. These prophets were men who saw what nobody else saw, heard what nobody else heard, and felt what nobody else felt. They lived in such close communion with God that it seemed he spoke to them, and what he spoke, they communicated to man. So it is that you read, "The word of the Lord came to Jeremiah. . . . The word of the Lord came to Ezekiel. . . . The word of the Lord came to Amos." But the words of God were not enough; the question remained unanswered and the wistfulness remain unresolved.

The reason for that is very simple. Words are such brittle things. They fall apart quickly. Words constantly change in meaning. Words have different meaning to different people. No two people give exactly the same shade of interpretation to the same word. Just walk down Broadway with the word "democracy," and see how far you get. Besides, it is very hard to put some ideas into words. Language has a way of breaking down. Words are not big

110

enough to hold the meaning. That is especially true in the spiritual world. Divine truth can never be petrified into a fixed form. You cannot confine it within the wall of words. The finite can never hold the infinite.

There are certain ideas which can never be known or understood through words. They must be felt and lived and experienced. Ideas must be embodied in personality to give them meaning. Words like holiness, love, and virtue cannot be understood apart from character. They have value only when somebody lives them. One day Josiah Royce was sitting in his study in Cambridge with a Harvard freshman. In the course of the conversation the young student asked the professor, "What is your definition of a Christian?" The great philosopher looked out of the window and said to the student, "I do not know what is the definition of a Christian, but there goes Phillips Brooks." You see, certain ideas must be felt and lived to be understood.

Words, therefore, are never enough, not even God's words. So through the ages men continued their plaintive call, "Oh that I knew where I might find him." Then in the fullness of time God sent his Son. Thus "the word was made flesh, and dwelt among us, . . . full of grace and truth." When men saw Jesus and looked into his face they shouted, "Emmanuel, God with us." When people asked Jesus what God was like, he replied, "I am the way, the truth, and the life; no man cometh unto the Father but by me." "He that hath seen me hath seen the Father." The unknown writer of the almost forgotten book of the Hebrews begins, "God who at sundry times and in diverse manners spake in time past unto the fathers by the prophets,

111

hath in these last days spoken unto us by his Son." That is the meaning of the Incarnation.

So it was that Jesus introduced a new idea into religion. It was as if he said, "God can only be made known and real when he is incarnated." Mankind will never find its way to him by creeds but by character; not through debates but through demonstrations; not by promises but by personalities; not by words but by life. God will be understood when men live him. The Word must always be made flesh and dwell among us.

That was true of the early Church. The most striking characteristic of first-century Christianity was its contagion. Nothing can match the miraculous growth and the expansion of the fellowship of Jesus in that era. The unfriendliness of public opinion, the venom of religious bigotry, the pressure of social ostracism, and the casualness of political leaders were their day-by-day experience. And yet, within three centuries they brought some three million converts into the Church; turned the world upside down and inside out; and carried the gates of the Roman Empire from their hinges.

What explains all that, and how can you account for it? It did not come to pass through organization. They did not employ artists to draw posters or psychologists to break down sales resistance or economists to draw graphs or Gallup polls to measure public opinion. Again, you cannot explain it on the basis of creed. There was among them no agreement in every detail of faith. They had no common statement or creed. What we put first they did not think important enough to put last. Nor can you explain it on the

112

basis of a common ritual. Aesthetic loveliness and ecclesiastical millinery meant little to them. They preferred to drink spring water out of a rusted dipper rather than vinegar out of a golden chalice. What, then, explains it?

There is no explanation for this phenomenal advance save in this fact: They walked into their world with souls made radiant and transformed by the impact of Jesus. They lived their religion. They bore branded on their bodies the marks of the Lord Jesus. Paul spoke for them, "The life which I now live, . . . I live by the faith of the Son of God, who loved me, and gave himself for me." They went up and down saying, "That which we have seen and heard declare we unto you." Their testimony was, "Whereas I was blind, now I see." They showed their generation what Christ had done for them, and could do for all men everywhere. They did not offer their generation an argument, but the alluring loveliness of a Christ-filled spirit. They changed their world, not by what they said, but by what they were. "The Word was made flesh, and dwelt among us."

If ever the appalling wistfulness of our time is to be resolved, and if ever the kingdom of God is to come among men, it will be when we have recovered that way of witness. Religion, to be real, must burn like a torch and shine like a star. One of the regrettable blunders and fallacies of so much endeavor to build the kingdom of God and bring in a new order is to suppose you can advance it by words. We have been going to men with statements of faith and doctrines, embossed resolutions and creeds. If words could transform men, this earth would be paradise. You can never redeem or transform men by a syllogism. They need something more than an argument.

Words have never attracted men to religion; rather they have repelled men. Words have never united the fellowship of Jesus; they have only divided it. Words have become walls instead of windows, barriers rather than bridges. Words are cheap and meaningless and empty. Chesterton once made the interesting observation that in the first century Christianity was advanced by Christians who practiced it; in later centuries they tried to advance it by debating it because that was easier. Dr. John Whale, one of our distinguished Christian scholars, in one of his recent books recalls the legend of a man who died and was carried to the gates of heaven. There he saw two entrances. Over one was written "This Is Heaven," and over the other was written "Discussion About Heaven"; and he saw that everybody was trying to get in by the second gate. That is still so today.

You cannot suppose that by speaking in a certain way about religion you advance religion. Indeed, Christianity is not so much a way of thinking as it is a way of living; it is not a religion, it is a life. There are many of my generation who bewail the loss of interest in the Church on the part of many of this present generation. Indeed, they are apt to look down their noses at them. When you honestly try to find the reason for that, you will discover it is not due to the fact that this generation has lost concern for the kingdom of God or fails to appreciate the glory of Christ, but rather that those who profess to be his disciples fail to incarnate him in their day-by-day lives. When I was a young man, I was almost kept out of the Church because there lived in my community a man who had all the answers. He could argue every doctrine with a hairsplitting finesse, but you could not trust him with a nickel. He was always trying to underchange and overcharge humble and poor people. The things we say about religion must somehow conform to the way we live with religion if anything is to come of it. When there is a contradiction between the words we speak and the lives we live, nothing can come of it.

Christ has not called us to defend him; he can defend himself; he has called us to demonstrate him and proclaim him. A religion of words divorced from life is like a man in a motorcar with his engine racing, but getting nowhere because it is never thrown into gear. Is it not time for Christian people to come down out of their stratosphere of abstraction? It is literally true that faith without works is dead.

Now a religion based only on words always breaks down in a crisis. One often comes upon people today who have been overwhelmed by some untoward circumstance with which they cannot cope. Suddenly their lives tumble apart and the lamps begin to flicker. The first thing these people are apt to do is to turn religion out of their lives and toss their faith out of the window. They give up all belief just at a time when they need it most. When you sit down with people like that and ask them why they followed that course, you will discover that they had a religion of a kind, but it did not go very deep. Their religion was a pose or a façade—it did not go down to the roots of conduct or character. If religion is to be genuine, it ought to have some effect upon the way we live.

There is a vast difference between religion and theology, which we often overlook. Religion is an experience which men have with God. Theology is the attempt to express that experience in words. But when people think more of the expression than of the experience, something goes out of their lives. A person may know all about Christianity, but that does not make him a Christian. The greatest single barrier to the coming of the kingdom of Christ is that we have too many people who give it intellectual assent but who fail to bear witness to it in their day-by-day conduct.

The man who recites the creed, burns his candles, chants his prayers, but who loses his temper every time he trips over a rug or curses the day he was born when he fails to catch a bus, who shortchanges and overcharges, and is calloused and unconcerned in his contact with man, is a hindrance and barrier to the kingdom of God. Those who have done most for the advancement of Christian faith have always been numbered among those in whom the word became flesh. The greatest single contribution which anyone can make to the building of a Christian order is to incarnate the life and teachings of Jesus in day-by-day life. Christianity does bring joy, peace, and strength, but it cannot prove its claim until somebody lives it and makes it real in his life.

It all comes back to this: What is your religion? Is it a voice or is it an echo? Is it a conviction or is it an opinion? Is it an experience or is it an argument? Did you get it out of a book or did you get it out of life? "Sayest thou this thing of thyself, or did others tell it thee of me?" That is the final witness of the Christian minister.

There are the lines of John Drinkwater:

> We know the paths wherein our feet should press;
> Across our hearts are written Thy decrees;
> Yet now, O Lord, be merciful to bless
>   With more than these.
>
> .   .   .   .
>
> Knowledge we ask not—knowledge Thou hast lent;
> But, Lord, the will—there lies our bitter need;
> Give us to build above the deep intent
>   The deed, the deed.

VIII. *The Fellowship of the Cross*

THE CHRISTIAN CHURCH IS SUFFERING FROM A DISCIPLESHIP which has lost faith in its enterprise. The defeatist spirit is commonplace among us today. There is something disquieting about Protestantism in its constant and cynical self-criticism. We sing rather loudly about our achievements but all too often it is a mere whistling to keep up our courage. There are many who believe in it, never shrinking, never faltering, standing face forward, but sometimes it is with the attitude of "We who are about to die, salute you." The cruel observation of Marcus Aurelius is haunting too many people in the Church, "This too, will pass away." Here and there you will find a man, blessed be God, who stands unashamed and unafraid with the radiance of the dawn upon him. But such spirits are rare. Indeed, they are like islands of hope in a sea of cynicism.

That is especially true in the Protestant Church. There are those who apologize for it but do not defend it. They have an idea that the less said about it, the better. They think of it as something quite negative, crying down this or that. It seems always to be against something. It has no positive or constructive contribution to make. They fear that the birth of the Protestant Church was a blunder. It

118

stands for nothing in particular. They think of the Reformation as a great mistake set off by a group of intellectual incendiaries and religious fanatics. They think it would never have come to pass if wiser and saner men had been in command. They gladly admit that while Protestantism once had a place and a mission, it no longer has a functioning purpose in society. In a day when individual freedom was to the fore, it served a purpose, but in this more complex and complicated age of co-operative movements it just has no message. It does not fit into these times.

Two thousand years ago a handful of frustrated, despairing men, haunted by terrifying misgivings, slinked through the winding streets of old Jerusalem to the upper room of a widow's home. There the divine afflatus settled upon them and the Holy Ghost came to them. At once they became as men transformed. They went back into a world which hated them, laughing at persecution, unperturbed by cross-bearing. The people who walk through the New Testament are gallant souls. They lived with a kind of divine nonchalance. They were fired with a great faith. They left behind two great words which they flung across the pages of the New Testament: "Abba," Father, and "Maranatha," Jesus come. By these two words their lives were transformed, and they changed their generation.

One does not often meet such men today, nor does one hear these words very often. In his illuminating and penetrating treatise on the meaning of religion Tolstoy suggests that in all human societies at certain periods of time, religion swerves from its original purpose, diverges more and more from what is central, until finally it petrifies into fixed forms so that its influence becomes less and less, and in the end a growing minority ceases to believe in it, and the masses are no longer guided by it. The Christian Church faces that peril in this hour. We need to hear the sharp warning of John in his Revelation as he stood upon the beetling cliffs of Patmos, "Repent . . . do first the works . . . or else I will remove thy candlesticks."

When we try to find the reason for that carping and critical attitude to the Church, we are reminded of the discouraging and disheartening estrangements of Christendom. It seems as if everybody is writing or saying something about the hapless and hopeless divisions in the Christian religion. Much is made of them both by friend and foe. What should be a uniting force has actually become an element of estrangement. What was designed to bind men together has actually repelled men from one another. No quarrels are so deep as those between religious men. Indeed, there is so much emphasis on the forces that have driven Christendom apart that many people on the outside think of Christianity in terms of divisiveness.

Finding fault with the Church has become the favorite indoor sport of those who are dedicated to defend it. Sometimes when I hear men decry the Church, look down their noses at its shortcomings and inconstancies, which we all regret, I want to raise my voice and cry out, "You who find fault with what it does, but do not lift hands to correct, how good must the Church be before you condescend to give your name to it?" I am quite sure that people on the outside will never stop throwing stones at it until people on the inside stop making light of it.

Now no one would question the existence of this divisiveness in Christendom. It is regrettably true that we seem to hate a shade of truth more than we hate error. We have emphasized areas of disagreement rather than the beliefs we share. These endless and increasing divisions are a source of weakness. We are not particularly proud of them. Just as families cannot achieve happiness while brother hates brother and daughter disavows parent, so in the Christian Church there cannot be unity of spirit while these differences are emphasized and intensified. A divided Church can never heal a divided world. If the world is to be one, the Christian Church must set a better example.

No man has ever built a fence so high and so wide but that he shut out infinitely more than he shut in. In climbing mountains one soon discovers that at the foot of the mountain, roads and trails are far apart, but the nearer you come to the top, the closer are the roads together until at last they all meet at the peak. That is another way of saying that the sense of oneness in the Church increases in proportion as we are near to Christ. The farther we get away from him the more do men drift apart. We all, therefore, regret these areas of estrangement in the Church. We have seemingly forgotten the prayer of our Lord, "That they all may be one, . . . that the world may believe that thou has sent me."

While no one can question what I have said, there are, however, certain facts of which the average layman is apt to lose sight. It is well to bear in mind that the divisions of

121

Protestantism began in a perfectly normal and natural way. The Reformation expressed itself in Germany through Lutheranism, in Scotland through Presbyterianism, in England through the Episcopacy and later through Methodism, and on the Continent through the Reformed Church. These were simply expressions of the same fundamental movement upon the background of differing national and racial patterns. I am not now, of course, referring to the numberless splinter groups, but rather to those major divisions of Protestantism at the time of its birth. In due time people who lived with these expressions immigrated into this country and established those expressions of the Protestant Church with which they had grown up.

Then, too, it is well to bear in mind that Protestantism has never believed in uniformity; it has, however, concerned itself with unity. Uniformity is a thing on the surface. It is external. Unity is a thing of the spirit; it is inward and born of the soul. It is not uniformity which the Protestant Church seeks, but something much deeper: a unity of the spirit. I do not belong to those who decry the existence of different approaches and different patterns in Christian faith. Sunshine falling on the fields of Kansas brings wheat; sunshine falling upon the fertile land of California makes roses; sunshine falls upon the fields of Dixie, and you have cotton. So it is with this matter of faith. It is so easy to confuse uniformity and unity. There is something to be said for these varying expressions of Protestant Christianity.

Those who think of the Church only in terms of disagreement and estrangement are apt to be superficial judges.

It is so easy to exaggerate differences and lose sight of the overtones of good will which exist. This constant emphasis upon the lack of oneness in the Christian Church loses sight of one fundamental fact. No one can deny that there are vast areas of disagreement, but there is also a fundamental area of agreement. And the things in which Christendom everywhere is in agreement are much more fundamental, significant, and permanent than the things in which there is disagreement.

There is often an ugly and regrettable mood in human nature. So often people see only what is not there, rather than what is there. They think only of what does not exist, rather than what does exist. We read a book and remember only the occasional grammatical error or imperfect development of some minor character in the plot. We go to an art gallery and remember only the flaw in one picture in some corner of one alcove. We go to a concert and recall only the one measure in which the strings were out of tune. A man may be a saint in patience, but let him show one evidence of petulance and he is tumbled from his pedestal. A man may walk in integrity all his days, but let him in a moment of weakness yield to one temptation, and that is all people will remember. For more than two thousand years the Christian Church has been in the world enriching its art and culture, transforming its society, and changing people into new patterns. Yet after all these generations of transforming and enriching life, men see only its foibles. What I am trying to say is that for all the disagreements and tensions there are also areas of oneness which are much more significant and abiding.

But how can the Church increase this needed unity of spirit? In the attempt to resolve these many estrangements and bring Christendom to a new sense of oneness many proposals have been made and many methods have been employed. We are all agreed that something must be done about it. The methods, however, of ridding the Church of this unhealthy state of affairs are often disappointing. There are those who say that if we could force upon all the differing groups one common creed or one common statement of faith, then the problem would be solved and the day of tension and strain would end. Many have tried to find some least common denominator of belief which would be acceptable to all varying groups. They have directed their attention to writing a statement of faith which would be least objectionable to the entire fellowship. They want to water down all these doctrinal statements and beliefs. But you can never make the Church one by forcing it to accept a common creed. Words do not unite men but divide men. Keeping religion in the realm of an intellectual approach only has never advanced the cause of Christ. Listen to an early Church leader writing in A.D. 406: "Since the Niceaen Creed we have done nothing but write creeds. We fight about creeds, contend over statements, take advantage of ambiguities and prepare anathemas. Yet there is scarcely a man who belongs to God." A vibrant and vital Church will never recover its unity by forcing people to live under the strait jacket of a common creed.

Then, too, many have thought that we could put an end to this deplorable divisiveness in Christendom if we would all unite in some common program. That seems to be the favorite technique today. If we can get people to become absorbed in some common tasks, then they will forget about their religious differences. It is a point of view which makes a church a fellowship of well-wishers, a company of busybodies running about furiously upon this or that errand. As if beliefs do not matter. If that is to be our procedure, what becomes of our convictions? It is true, of course, that the Church must come out of the stratosphere of abstraction and integrate its convictions into contemporary life, but you can't make a tree healthy by pruning the branches and spraying the leaves only. If you fail to feed the roots or nourish the soil in which it grows, the tree will sooner or later wither. The roots of the Church are planted in the soil of a living faith and when that soil becomes sour, the tree, too, will perish for all our pruning. It is so easy to make secondary things primary and primary things secondary. We are so apt to take the things that lie in the center and push them beyond the circumference and take the things that lie on the fringes and push them in the center.

All this involves the Church in an endless series of unrelieved trivialities: beautiful form, attractive liturgy, and ecclesiastical millinery. Often attractive ritual has been made not an aid to religion but a substitute for it. The Church is praised for its music, admired for its architecture, and applauded for its equipment. The Church can never be made vital and vibrant by emphasis upon program and technique only. You can never heal the discouraging and disheartening estrangements which exist in the Church by compromise or by program.

125

I venture to suggest what is needed to bring to the Church a new oneness of mind and heart is a return to that which lies at the center of our common faith. We must make more of the Cross. I would like to remind you that while we have many statements of faith, we have only one gospel. We have many ministers but only one Saviour. We have many altars but only one Lamb of God. We have many creeds but only one Cross.

It is the Cross which stands central in the faith of Christendom. John the Baptist pointed to it when he said, "Behold the Lamb of God, which taketh away the sin of the world." Paul went up and down Asia Minor proclaiming the simple resolve: "God forbid that I should glory, save in the cross of our Lord Jesus Christ." John laid bare the heart of the gospel, "For God so loved the world, that he gave his only begotten Son." Jesus made that Cross central in all his preaching and teaching. He came to the end of the end, and you hear him say, "And I, if I be lifted up from the earth, will draw all men unto me." George Bernard Shaw once said, "Jesus of Nazareth was crucified upon a thin stick of wood, but he had a strange way of getting hold of it at the right end."

The early Church was held together by keeping that Cross central. What a strange and complex group it was. These early Christians represented different nationalities with different languages, different traditions, different types of organizations and with different creedal statements. You come upon the fickle Galatians; there were the wayward Romans; you meet the warmhearted Philippians; there were the unpredictable and unstable Thessalonians.

And yet, all these differing groups with their different patterns were held together in one great fellowship because their common gospel was, "he loved me and gave himself for me." "God forbid that I should glory, save in the cross of our Lord Jesus Christ."

That is still so today. The areas of estrangement and tension in Christendom are always in the direction of creeds. The increasing sense of oneness is always in the direction of the Cross. Wherever the Cross ceases to be central, Christendom has become weak, quarrelsome, and divided. The way back to oneness is by kneeling again in reverence and confession before the Cross. Our Lord himself must have anticipated this tendency to divisiveness when he urged the commandment, "This do in remembrance of me." Fearing that his disciples might fall apart into broken and brittle groups, he urged them to remember his Cross to the end of the end. You don't have to be afraid of differences of opinion which men may hold in the Christian Church so long as they can sing together:

> When I survey the wondrous cross
> On which the Prince of Glory died,
> My richest gain I count but loss,
> And pour contempt on all my pride.

When Christian people everywhere, with all their varying statements of faith and tensions, emphasize again this central fact of our gospel, most of its disagreements will be resolved. The nearer we are to the Cross, the nearer will we be to one another. Kneeling at the foot of Calvary has a way of resolving all differences. They no longer seem important. Indeed, we no longer take note of them. You just can't hate people with whom you kneel before the Cross of Christ.

No one has a monopoly upon that Cross. It is meant for all: Catholic and Calvinist; Quaker and Anglican; Baptist and Presbyterian and Methodist. That Cross has always brought people together. A Calvinist wrote, "Rock of Ages;" it was a Congregationalist who sang, "My Faith Looks Up to Thee"; a Methodist has spoken for us all in the hymn, "Jesus, Lover of My Soul"; a Scotch Presbyterian wrote, "I Heard the Voice of Jesus Say"; a parish priest sang, "Jesus, the Very Thought of Thee," a monk in the long-ago centuries added, "Art Thou Weary, Art Thou Troubled?" It was a Quaker who sang, "Drop Thy still dews of quietness till all our strivings cease." Everywhere, up and down Christendom, Christian men and women sing these hymns together. The Cross always brings into being a new sense of oneness.

Do you know the story of the soldier on the Anzio beachhead? After that dreadful and bloody break-through, our troops liberated rather quickly one Italian village after another. Late one afternoon they had captured an almost deserted small village. When the fighting was over, one of our soldiers walked back through the main street of the village to what was left of the parish church, which had been ruthlessly bombed. He stumbled over a rubble pile at the entrance and walked down the center aisle until he stood face to face with the symbolism of everything he held dear, and by which he lived. As he stood there alone, he heard another G.I. come stumbling over the rubble pile and walk down the center aisle. The second soldier had come from a first-aid station. He had been wounded in both arms, which were bound together in a sling. He told the first soldier that he had come there to pray, but he could not. When he was asked why he could not pray, he said he was a Catholic and could not make the sign of the Cross. The first soldier said to him that he was a Protestant but that he believed also in Christ and the Cross. Would he do? So the two of them kneeled side by side and the Protestant made for the Catholic the sign of the Cross. Each prayed to God in his own way. When the Protestant boy got up, he said that he found himself crying. He looked out of the corner of his eye, and he saw that the Catholic soldier was crying too. Then, writing the incident later in a letter, he added, "I wonder if God was crying too; I think he was."

The Cross has a strange way of bringing about a sense of oneness even against our own designs. When the Cross comes back into the consciousness and witness of the Church, it will have not only a new oneness but a new power. Paul spoke for the whole of Christendom when he said, "God was in Christ, reconciling the world unto himself."

In the National Gallery in London there is a dramatic picture which I have often seen. As you come upon it, it seems a mere blending of shadows and darkness. Nothing seems to break the unrelieved night. As you walk a little closer, you see vaguely the outline of a cross hidden behind the veil of shadows. Then as you look a little longer, you become strangely aware that behind the cross you see the dim outlines of a figure with hands outstretched, holding that cross, and the agony on the face hidden by the shadows

129

is more terrible than the agony of the face of him who hangs on the cross. There you have in art the meaning and the power of the Cross which draws all men. Peter spoke a strange phrase on the day of Pentecost: "Him, being delivered up by the determinate counsel and foreknowledge of God." For a long time it was to me a very disturbing sentence, but it is profound and a revealing truth. Whatever else it may mean, it means surely this: God was not asleep when Jesus died. He was not an indifferent spectator to the suffering of his Son. The reins had not slipped out of his hand. Calvary did not make the love of God, but the love of God made Calvary. The Cross was not an accident. Through it our Lord seemed to say, "You can do with me what you like; you can break my bones and drain my blood and bruise my flesh, but you can't stop me from loving you." "Having loved his own which were in the world, he love them unto the end."

That needs saying with all the compassion and all the urgency at our command. If that Cross could become again central in our witness, believe me, a new sense of oneness would come to the Church and a new hope would come to our disillusioned generation. I do not quarrel with men who have an imperfect view of the Cross. Who can ever understand its mystery? Human understanding can never fathom its depth. But I quarrel with men who preach no Cross at all.

Some time ago a distinguished professor of one of our leading theological seminaries was talking with me about modern preaching. He was very critical of it, and thought it very shallow and shoddy. I asked him what he thought was the reason. He replied rather solemnly, "We no longer know what the gospel is. Modern preaching has lost all too often its message."

There was that day long ago on a hill called Golgotha. The multitudes crowded close to him, reviling him and saying, "If thou be the Son of God, come down from the cross, and we will believe thee." How often we hear that today. Come down from the Cross, come down to our level, come down to what we think is important, and we will be your disciples. How very often, too, he has been taken down from the Cross and presented to men as one who had not died. There is no chance for such a gospel. It is only when we exalt the Cross that there will come to the fellowship of Jesus a new witness, a new sense of oneness, and a new message of hope for our blundering age.

Dr. Robert Norwood, one of the distinguished preachers of New York of the last generation, told an interesting experience of his early ministry. He had finished his theological training and was going home to spend a week end with his father, who was the rector of a humble parish church in Maine. He was to preach his first sermon. When he arrived, Robert Norwood thought that his father would ask him what he planned to preach about. But all that long Saturday night his father said nothing about it. The next morning at breakfast there was no reference to the sermon. As they put on their vestments he thought his father would say something about it, but not a word was spoken. He preached the sermon, and afterward they went home, but the father made no comment on it. They drove out into the country that afternoon, but again, there was no men-tion of the sermon. Nothing was said of it in the evening. The next day Robert Norwood was going to the train to return to the seminary. He wondered why it was that his father made no comment on the sermon. As the carriage came near to the station, Robert Norwood turned to his father and said, "Father, what did you think about my sermon? You have said nothing about it so far." The father stopped the carriage, turned to his son, and said, "Robert, when you preach, you either stand in front of the Cross or behind the Cross. Giddyap."

Many statements of faith, only one gospel; many ministers and priests, only one Saviour; many altars, only one Lamb of God; many creeds, only one Cross. So he stands at his Cross, the strong among the weak, the erect among the fallen, the pure among the unclean, the believing among the doubting, the confident among the confused. That Cross is the answer to every dilemma and every disillusionment, whether international, economic, social, political, or personal. The world is not done with the Cross, but the world is done without it. Preach it. You did not make it, neither can you change it. The heart of the world is turning to that gospel. God forbid we should trail in the dust men's golden hopes.

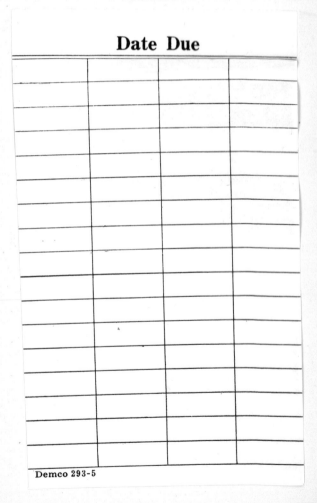

Date Due